NO LONGER PROPERTY OF
LONG BEACH PUBLIC LIBRARY

Can I Get a Witness?

Other books by Brian K. Blount
from Westminster John Knox Press

Preaching Mark in Two Voices, with Gary W. Charles

Struggling wth Scripture, with Walter Brueggeman and William C. Placher

Making Room at the Table: An Invitation to Multicultural Worship, with Leonora Tubbs Tisdale, eds.

DURNETT

Can I Get a Witness?

Reading Revelation through African American Culture

Brian K. Blount

WESTMINSTER
JOHN KNOX PRESS
LOUISVILLE • KENTUCKY

© 2005 Brian K. Blount

All rights reserved. No part of this book may be reproduced or transmitted in any form or by any means, electronic or mechanical, including photocopying, recording, or by any information storage or retrieval system, without permission in writing from the publisher. For information, address Westminster John Knox Press, 100 Witherspoon Street, Louisville, Kentucky 40202-1396.

Scripture quotations from the New Revised Standard Version of the Bible are copyright © 1989 by the Division of Christian Education of the National Council of the Churches of Christ in the U.S.A. and are used by permission.

Every effort has been made to trace the owner or holder of each copyright. If any rights have been inadvertently infringed upon, the publisher asks that the omission be excused and agrees to make the necessary corrections in subsequent printings. Excerpts from "The Symphony" by Kirby Spivey III are reprinted by permission. Excerpt from *Why Lord? Suffering and Evil in Black Theology*, by Anthony B. Pinn. Copyright © 1995 by Continuum Publishing Co. Reprinted by permission of Continuum Publishing Co. Excerpts from "Party for Your Right to Fight" by Eric D. Sadler, James Henry Boxley III, Carlton Douglas Ridenhour, George Clinton Jr., Edwared Earl Hazel, and Bernard Worrell. Copyright © 1988 Songs of Universal, Inc. on behalf of Def American songs, Inc. All rights reserved. Used by permission of Universal Music Publishing Group. Also copyright 1988 by Bridgeport Music Inc. (BMI)/Southfield Music Inc. (and co-publishers). All rights reserved. Used by permission of Bridgeport Music Inc. and Southfield Music Inc. Also copyright © 1988 Reach Global Songs (BMI), a division of Reach Global, Inc. [and other publishers]. Used by permission of Reach Global, Inc. Excerpt from "God Bless the Dead" by Tupac Amaru Shakur and Duane Nettlesby. Copyright © 1998 Songs of Universal, Inc. on behalf of itself and Joshua's Dream Music. All rights reserved. Used by permission of Universal Music Publishing Group and Warner Bros. Publications U.S. Inc., Miami, Florida 33014. Excerpts from "Hail Mary" by Tupac Amaru Shakur, Bruce Washington, Yafeu A. Fula, Katari Cox, Rufus Cooper, Joseph Paquette, and Tyrone J. Wrice. Copyright © 1996 Songs of Universal, Inc. on behalf of itself and Joshua's Dream Music and Gimme Minz Publishing and Royal Safari Music/Universal Music Corp. on behalf of itself and Yaki Kadafi Music and Thug nation Music and Foxbeat Music. All rights reserved. Used by permission of Universal Music Publishing Group and Warner Bros. Publications U.S. Inc., Miami, Florida 33014. Excerpts from "Unconditional Love" by Tupac Amaru Shakur and Johnny Jackson. Copyright © 1998 Songs of Universal, Inc. on behalf of itself and Joshua's Dream Music. All rights reserved. Used by permission of Universal Music Publishing Group and Warner Bros. Publications U.S. Inc., Miami, Florida 33014. Excerpts from "Proud to Be Black" by Joseph Simmons and Darryl McDaniels. Copyright © 1986 Rabasse Music Ltd. and Rush Groove Music. All rights reserved. Used by permission of Warner Bros. Publications U.S. Inc., Miami, Florida 33014. Excerpts from the Rev. Dr. Martin Luther King Jr. are reprinted by arrangement with the Estate of Martin Luther King Jr., c/o Writers house as agent for the proprietor, New York, NY. Copyright 1968 Martin Luther King Jr., copyright renewed 1999 Coretta Scott King.

Book design by *Sharon Adams*
Cover design by *designpointinc.com*
Cover photo: *Civil Rights March Across Selma Bridge* © *Flip Schulke/CORBIS*

First edition
Published by Westminster John Knox Press
Louisville, Kentucky

This book is printed on acid-free paper that meets the American National Standards Institute Z39.48 standard. ∞

PRINTED IN THE UNITED STATES OF AMERICA

05 06 07 08 09 10 11 12 13 14—10 9 8 7 6 5 4 3 2 1

Library of Congress Cataloging-in-Publication Data

Blount, Brian K.
    Can I get a witness? : reading Revelation through African American culture / Brian K. Blount.
        p. cm.
    Includes bibliographical references.
    ISBN 0-664-22869-0 (alk. paper)
    1. Bible. N.T. Revelation—Criticism, interpretation, etc. 2. Christianity and culture. 3. African Americans—Religion. I. Title.
BS2825.52.B56 2005
228'.06—dc22   2004054949

3 3090 00403 8909

Contents

Introduction

I did not come to my current fascination with Revelation naturally. Very little about the book speaks to the Christian interests that orient and shape my life. Or so I once thought. During my one year as educator and six years as pastor of an African American Presbyterian church, I do not remember teaching or preaching out of the text more than once. On that single occasion, I believe I was drawn to the images of the new heaven and new earth as a metaphorical way of celebrating and, perhaps more importantly, encouraging the church's foray into a long needed, but expensive building program. I otherwise managed successfully to avoid any entanglements with it. As an academic at Princeton Theological Seminary, where I find myself part of a large and talented biblical studies department, I have been blessed with the luxury of teaching and researching in areas that interest me most. Until a few years ago, I have not been "most interested" in studying the Apocalypse. While I am obliged to teach certain required courses, no one has ever demanded that I take it upon myself to extend my repertoire by engaging John's Patmos visions.

My interests have been those of culture and the influence of culture on the reading of biblical materials. Of those materials, I have been drawn to the Synoptic Gospels. I have tried to develop methodologies that would allow me to read the Gospels from my cultural context as an African American Christian. I have been just as interested, though, in understanding how my own readings can and do differ from those of persons in contexts that are not my own. And so I have also happily expended a great deal of energy working through the interpretive methods of sociolinguistics and cultural hermeneutics. I have, in other words, been trying to find a way to analyze exactly how the background that we bring with us to the reading of biblical texts influences the decisions we end up making about what those texts mean.

Who knows what Revelation means? Perhaps that ambiguity, which seems to remain even after one studies the book under the tutelage of multiple commentaries and other interpretive materials, is one of the reasons I neglected the work. I am not one who enjoys the kind of puzzling narrative portrait that John delighted in painting. I am also not inclined toward the reading of materials that I find distasteful. Revelation's misogynist reputation and its penchant for graphic violence were other reasons why I chose not to locate a great deal of my interpretive energies there. I remember quite vividly a conversation I had a year ago with an Old Testament colleague at a meeting of the Society of Biblical Literature. After I told him that I had been invited to do a commentary on the Apocalypse, he lectured me quite vigorously about the need to tell the "truth" about the book's less than generous characterization of women and its unholy presentation of a violent God bent on revenge. My lifelong affiliation with the church and my appreciation for its biblical record make me hesitant about challenging texts that I hold to be authoritative. And yet, because of my academic training, I do not want to position myself as an uncritical defender of those biblical words that do disservice to the Word of God they try narratively to convey. Revelation, therefore, presents itself as a unique challenge. It offers an apocalyptic window into both the Word of God and the sometimes troubling human words that John uses to convey what he sees.

In the end, it was that intriguing offer to do a commentary on the work that drew me cautiously into its literary orbit. The more I pored over the material, particularly from my conscious reading perspective as an African American Christian, the more intrigued I became. I was fascinated by the oppressive context in which John understood himself and his church to exist. I found in that context a provocative correspondence with the long-standing and long-suffering circumstance of the African American church. The invitation to do the commentary drew me to the work; the perceived correspondence between John's history and African American Church history convinced me to stay with it.

Commentaries, of course, take some time. While working on the details of that assignment, I have taken a very pleasant detour that has allowed me the opportunity to combine my interest in cultural interpretation with my developing work on the Apocalypse. That detour has led me to the materials that make up the chapters of this book. While working on Revelation from my cultural location, I have come to the conclusion that John was interested not so much in creating a church of martyrs as he was in encouraging a church filled with people committed to the ethical activity of witnessing to the lordship of Jesus Christ. On the surface, that sounds like an exclusively spiritual and pious act. In John's context, it was also a highly social, economic, and political one.

In John's Asia Minor location, the imperial cult had risen to an impressive social, religious, and political height. Pious proclamations about the divine status of the emperor, the Roman state, and their pagan divinities symbolized political allegiance to the empire. The more one accommodated oneself to such declarations and actions of allegiance, the more opportunity one had for advancement in the Roman-sponsored Asia Minor communities in which John's seven churches were located. Of course, the more one resisted such accommodation, the more one risked the ire of officials who were in Roman political employ. John asked his hearers and readers to live a life of just such resistance. He demanded that they refuse any opportunity, no matter how seemingly inconsequential, to acknowledge Roman imperial or pagan lordship. He demanded that they publicly and somewhat antagonistically witness to the lordship of Jesus Christ instead.

In a time and place where Christians were not subjected to a programmatic plan of persecution (as they had been during the time of the emperor Nero), but were often economically, socially, and even physically abused when they took it upon themselves to stand out and stand apart from the expected show of deference to Roman lordship, John was essentially asking his people to pick a social and religious fight. He was asking them to witness. It is that call for witness that energizes my work in this study.

This particular take obviously owes a great deal to my reading perspective. In order to help readers understand that perspective and why I believe it is important to engage Revelation (and all biblical materials) from such a perspective, I begin the work not with Revelation but with a study of the history of cultural studies. Following the work of Stephen Moore and others, I trace cultural studies from its genesis at the University of Birmingham to the unique brand of cultural inquiry that I find energizing in the United States. I try to demonstrate how much our reading conclusions about the book depend upon the cultural location from which we read it.

Having made that cultural case, I then strike out into the text of Revelation with African American culture as my reading lens. In the second chapter, I take on the language of "martyr" and argue that John intended it to mean just what it did mean in the first century: witness. Witnessing, not dying, was the goal John sought out for his hearers and readers. Witnessing was the ethic by which he wished them to live. I explore what that witnessing looked like as a social and political as well as spiritual endeavor for John's believers in the first century and what it looks like for Christian believers in the twenty-first century.

In the third chapter, "Wreaking Weakness: The Way of the Lamb," I revisit the Lamb metaphor. Arguing again from my cultural lens, I contend that John does not see the character sacrificially. The slaughtered Lamb is instead the prototypical witness figure, who models the ethic of confrontation that John expects from his own hearers and readers. Operating from the cultural observations of African American scholar Theophus Smith, I maintain that God deploys the violently slaughtered Lamb as a homeopathic cure for the very violence that slaughtered him and now threatens those who follow him.

In the fourth and final chapter, "The Rap against Rome: The Spiritual-Blues Impulse and the Hymns of Revelation," I consciously seek meaning from Revelation's hymns by reading them through the lens of the music that has been particularly important in African American culture: spirituals, gospel, blues, jazz, hip-hop, and rap. The thread of resistance to oppressive power that runs through John's hymns resonates with a parallel theme in the music of African America.

I am indebted to many colleagues and institutions who have helped me pursue my newfound interest in the Apocalypse. I am first of all thankful to John T. Carroll, Beverly Roberts Gaventa, and C. Clifton Black, the editors of Westminster John Knox's New Testament Library Series. If it were not for their very gracious invitation to do a commentary on Revelation, I am sure that I would not now be so engaged in its study. I am equally grateful for the invitation of the Centre for Studies in Religion and Society at the University of Victoria, in Victoria, British Columbia. Several years ago they invited me to do the John Albert Hall lectures, which were designed to engage scholars with issues of relevance for contemporary society. Their invitation provided me with the perfect opportunity to think about the book of Revelation from a contemporary cultural perspective. The chapters in this book are revised and lengthened versions of the lectures I gave to the academic and lay community at the Centre. I am honored to have been invited to take part in such a prestigious series. I thank Dr. Harold Coward for the initial invitation and Dr. Conrad Brunk, who took over as the Centre's director following Dr. Coward's retirement, for his warm and gracious hospitality during my time in Victoria. His assistance and the help of Leslie Kenny, administrator at the Centre, made my time there immensely profitable. Thanks, too, are due Moira C. Hill. Her e-mails and letters prepared me for my visit, and her generous spirit and attention to detail made me feel at home. I am also grateful for the questions and comments of the many persons who attended the lectures. They have helped me revise and rework the material in very helpful ways.

I add also a word of deep appreciation to Stephanie Egnotovich, my editor at Westminster John Knox. Her support for this work came at a particularly crucial and difficult time. Her professional guidance and her critical editorial eye have been treasured assets.

I also owe a debt of gratitude to my research assistant, Jacob Cherian. His assistance with editing and his work on the indexes have been invaluable.

I am finally very grateful for the institutional support offered by Princeton Theological Seminary and the Lilly Endowment. The sabbatical offered by Princeton allowed me to spend quality time doing research and writing for both the lecture and publication phases of the work. The funds I received as a Lilly Faculty Fellow made it possible to extend the single-semester sabbatical into a yearlong leave. With that extended time, I have had the opportunity to transition from my work on this project to concentrated work on the forthcoming commentary. In that work, too, I look forward to learning more about what I believe to be John's central petition to his seven Asia Minor churches: Can I Get a Witness?

Brian K. Blount
Princeton, NJ

Chapter 1

The Revelation of Culture

R evelation obscures. That is not, of course, John's intent. He seems to think he has cleared everything up. In picturing what God has revealed to him, he apparently presumes that he has clarified how believers are to live their lives. He is at his explanatory best in the opening three chapters. After capturing the imagination of his listeners with chapter 1's thrilling exposé of Jesus' cosmic power and eternal majesty, he turns to the mundane affairs of his all too fallible seven churches (2:1–3:22). A master motivator, he uses his images of the powerful and ever-present Christ to ratchet up feelings of devotion and obedience. His ethical mandates and pastoral castigations draw their strength from the carefully drawn revelation that Jesus is, always has been, and always will be Lord. His hearers and readers are to follow the ways of that Lord, witness to the rule of that Lord, suffer and die for the glory of that Lord, and believe in the imminent coming of that Lord to right the wrongs of history and vindicate the people who have suffered so tragically because of them. Above all, as the Lord's representatives, they are to initiate his victory by living out a witness of active and aggressive resistance against any power, human or supernatural, that would contest his lordship by establishing and promoting its own.

But it is just here, at the point where he should be his most clear, that the seer stumbles into the proverbially murky deep end.

Beginning in chapter 4, he ushers us into the heavens and reveals a barrage of otherworldly images that are supposed to have a decidedly this-worldly instructional impact. Impact to what end, though, we clearly do not know. Stunned by the visual onslaught, centuries of interpreters have squinted through John's dark looking glass in an often futile effort to determine exactly what this apocalypse really reveals about God's expectations for faithful discipleship.

It is crucial that we determine what John is saying about Jesus, since the expectations for our behavior as disciples are based on the revelation of his identity as Lord. But that is precisely why we have a problem. The shocking visions that constitute the bulk of John's work, chapters 4–22, while undeniably awe-inspiring, provoke many more questions than answers. The magisterial God whom John pictures, and the Lord Jesus who follows in God's imperial wake, are caught up in a vengeful, misogynistic, hyperviolent, genocidal war whose cataclysms devour entire swathes of human, environmental, and cosmic being. What can that possibly mean for how humans are to live their lives as followers of that Lord? Can this Lord and the God he brings to life be the ones we are to emulate? Instead of clarifying, this Revelation obscures. It obscures God's intent for human involvement in the maelstrom leading up to and ultimately climaxing the end of time.

Fortunately for us, culture reveals. By enveloping an object of interpretation the way a carefully selected frame surrounds and thereby shapes the reading of the portrait it holds, culture contributes to meaning even as, and precisely because, it supplies context.[1] The revelation here is that the cultural context of the interpreter plays a powerful role in shaping the meaning that interpreter builds from his or her interaction with a text like John's Apocalypse.

Language is the foundation of every text. Language is potential. Language creates choice. It provides both the persons who draft it and those who subsequently encounter it with the opportunity to decode its audible sounds and visible markers. Words, for example, do not convey meaning; they convey meaning potential. That potential, that opportunity for choice, becomes *meaningful* only when it is performed and accessed in a certain context.

One might consider the example *head*. Clearly polyvalent, it could refer as easily to the leader of some organization or group as to the body part occupying the space between your shoulders. In some colloquial settings it could even be paired synonymously with as unlikely a partner as *bean* or *noggin*. A sailor in search of a particular kind of relief might access it in a totally different manner still.

In such a way, the single word attracts many different but still "correct" decoding choices. The "meaningful" choice depends on the context. Each word, then, is like a prism whose shape allows the refraction of many colors. The color or colors you see will change, depending on your position and the position, angle, and source of the light interacting with the prism.

If words are by themselves this polyvalent, one can imagine that the potential for meaning will increase exponentially as we collect words into sentences, sentences into paragraphs, and paragraphs into entire texts. The boundaries of choice widen even further in poetic texts, where an author *intends* that his or her words accommodate a high degree of symbolic elasticity. The language of apocalyptic, John's language in Revelation, is consciously poetic. Symbolic to the core, it invites choice at almost every linguistic turn.[2] The cultural space one occupies will therefore be a critical factor in determining how and what that language *means*.

No doubt this is why interpreters of historical critical persuasion have routinely anchored their interpretations of the Apocalypse in the presumed first-century cultural context of John and his first hearers/readers. The presumption is clear; John's writing context will clarify John's writing intent.

There are two problems. First, scholars don't *discover* John's culture. They reconstruct it. That reconstruction operates from historical and literary clues. John has embedded some of the most important of those clues in his writing. For example, he locates his churches in Asia Minor at a time when believers in the lordship of Jesus Christ were subject to varying forms of social and political hostility from those who represented the power, lordship, and influence of Rome. Such clues, however, are suggestive, not determinative. It is no wonder then that there has been considerable debate over John's *actual* historical circumstance. Was there a widespread pogrom against Christians, or was the hostility, while often deadly, sporadic and specifically targeted? Was Domitian the emperor of record? Or was John's Babylonian beast steered by some other shepherd? When even answers to such elementary questions are open to debate, it is clear that while the historical and literary clues offer meaning potential, they do not provide meaning, in the form of objective, historical fact. Historians and exegetes use that potential in their reconstructive efforts. They access that potential through the lens of their own historical, social, political, and religious cultural contexts. The end result? The context into which researchers situate and thereby shape their interpretation of John's Revelation is rigged as much by the presumptions of their own cultural locations as by any alleged historical *facts*.

The second problem derives from the first. Historical critical researchers presumed that the past meaning they divined from a careful consideration of John's Revelation in light of John's *historical* context would be the one objective meaning that was stable and therefore meaningful for every reader in every place and time. Ironically, this quest for *the* past meaning obscured the fact that different interpreters from different contemporary contexts were reading the literary and contextual signals differently. Even when historical critical interpreters were fortunate enough to come to some consensus about John's *historical* context, they still *found* different and often opposing *objective* meanings.[3] Why? Culture. Not John's culture. The Johannine interpreter's culture.

Culture reveals. Revelation *seen* (the Revelation we see) is always Revelation *read* (the Revelation we read) through a particular cultural lens. It is therefore the Revelation of and for a particular, *present* culture. If that is indeed the case, if—whether we want it to or not—culture plays a key role in the revelatory process, why not do a cultural studies reading of Revelation? Instead of clinging to a fruitless search for a universal, objective interpretation whose one counsel pretends to fit everyone in every conceivable context, why not deploy a cultural studies model that can clarify Revelation's meaning for *us* and reveal the kind of apocalyptic discipleship God expects from *us*?[4]

No matter what investigative methods are deployed, in the end a clear Revelation is always *our* Revelation. When we try to make someone else's Revelation *our* Revelation, that effort obscures and mystifies; it speaks to and for their culture, not ours. No wonder, then, that it so often ends up sounding like so much mythological mumbo jumbo. This is precisely why any critical attempt to locate the Apocalypse in its first-century context and then to divine *the* universal, objective meaning for the book out of that context is an abortive enterprise from the start. Even if an interpreter is so fortunate as to reconstruct John's first-century context with sharp historical accuracy, and is subsequently skilled enough to use some methodological apparatus to inoculate himself from his own cultural predispositions and influences, his objective, accurate reading of Revelation will still be obscure. It would not make sense to a twenty-first-century reader precisely because its sense would be permanently lodged in the cultural confines of the last decade of the first century (or whatever decade that proficient interpreter finally determined was the work's accurate date). That fortunate interpreter would find himself in possession of an interpretive fossil *from* some dead community in the past, not an instructive meaning *for* some particular living community in the present.

But that is, dare I say it, *good news*. A cultural studies approach to Revelation clarifies what is otherwise obscure and makes what is otherwise incomprehensible meaningful because it operates with a conscious degree of particularity. Culture reveals, specifically. A cultural reading reveals the meaning of Revelation for those who share its contextual dynamics. In other words, a cultural reading reveals what Revelation means *for us*. That does not mean that readers in other cultural contexts cannot find our conclusions helpful. A cultural reading of the Apocalypse not only brings new light to *our* understanding of Revelation; it does so in a way that appreciates how communal groups different from our own will draw their own culturally derived meaning conclusions. It subsequently fosters communication between us and them.

Readers learn more about Revelation when they listen to what people from other cultures have to say about the way Revelation reveals itself through the lens of their cultural encounter with it.

This is the paradox: Global comprehension of the book occurs only when readers surrender the quixotic quest for *the* one objective meaning that overrides all cultural limitations. Instead of immediately rejecting another culture's reading of the book as a corrupted, self-interested, and therefore biased eisegesis, the cultural reader recognizes that the only way to expand meaning is to value the fact that readers in different cultures will access meaning potential in ways that, while different, may well be no less worthy, no less meaningful.

This is *how* culture reveals. It is also *why* I want to pursue a cultural studies reading of Revelation. Given what I have just said, I obviously cannot do that by myself. I can only participate in what is by definition a joint process. I can start by reading Revelation from my own cultural location, allowing it in the process to clarify God's apocalyptic intent for my discipleship and the discipleship of those located with me. That meaning I will subsequently share with cultural Others. My research, then, does not intend to deliver *the* interpretive answer about the discipleship meaning of Revelation; it expects instead to initiate and benefit from an intercultural conversation. I therefore propose to use the cultural studies model to study the meaning of discipleship in Revelation through the lens of African American culture. I intend to offer that reading as another point of access to the meaning potential of Revelation. Before I can begin to do that, however, I must first define cultural studies, demonstrate its promise, and then share how it has already begun the conversational process of clarifying what has otherwise seemed quite obscure.

Cultural Studies: A Definition

The problem with defining cultural studies is that it resists definition. Its articulation as a plural noun is no mistake; it is not a single entity. In an academic world that rewards the meticulous scholar who works within the disciplined confines of a uniform analytical approach and punishes the one who does not, this poses a problem. John Storey is blunt: "The problem is this: cultural studies has never had one distinct method of approach to its object of study."[5]

"I want to insist on that!" Stuart Hall agrees. "[Cultural studies] had many trajectories; many people had and have different trajectories through it; it was constructed by a number of different methodologies and theoretical positions, all of them in contention."[6] Is the approach as disheveled as it sounds? Angela McRobbie not only thinks so; she appears to wallow exuberantly in the resulting mire. "Because, in my view, cultural studies was always messy. Characterized by intense internal theoretical conflict, it was also a messy amalgam of sociology, social history, and literature, rewritten as it were into the language of contemporary culture."[7] She goes on to say that cultural studies has been and should always be "a contested terrain of study. Not only contested but also resistant to disciplinary purity."[8] Why? Because there is a certain interpretive magic that happens as a result of methodological diversity. Freed from arbitrary methodological constraints, an interpreter has the freedom to match subjects of study with the methods of inquiry that fit them best. That interpreter also has the dexterity to make a methodological shift the moment a subject area declares itself resistant to whatever analytical approach is already underway. In this way, "Cultural Studies draws from whatever fields are necessary to produce the knowledge required for a particular project."[9]

The approach's ability to bridge the gulfs that divide interpretive communities is equally significant. Academic methodologies are themselves invested with the ideological interests of the academic communities that create and champion them. The selection of a particular methodology is therefore as much a political choice as it is an investigative one. By refusing to signal sole allegiance to any single approach, while simultaneously seeking the capabilities of every applicable one, cultural studies not only allows for the mixing of multiple ideological agendas in the interpretive process; it invites them. As Cary Nelson, Lawrence Grossberg, and Paula Treichler put it, "cultural studies holds special intellectual promise because it explicitly attempts to cut across diverse social and political interests."[10]

Multiform as it is, cultural studies maintains certain constants, traits and tendencies shared by its practitioners, that enable its identification as a single, if also dynamic, field. The first such shared trait is its very definition of the concept "culture." Raymond Williams, one of the early high priests of cultural studies, defined culture anthropologically, as "a particular way of life, whether of a people, a period or a group."[11] Succeeding scholars have been more specific. "In cultural studies traditions," Nelson, Grossberg, and Treichler explain, "culture is understood *both* as a way of life—encompassing ideas, attitudes, languages, practices, institutions, and structures of power—and a whole range of cultural practices: artistic forms, texts, canons, architecture, mass-produced commodities, and so forth."[12]

This particular way of everyday life and the practices attached to it are, for the purposes of these scholars, decidedly common. Just because a community has "culture" or is "cultured," so to speak, does not mean that it is therefore the object of cultural studies. In fact, that very high-end, euphemistic designation suggests that it explicitly is not. Storey is clear: "The object of study in cultural studies is not culture defined in the narrow sense, as the objects of aesthetic excellence ('high art'); nor culture defined in an equally narrow sense, as a process of aesthetic, intellectual and spiritual development; but culture understood as the texts and practices of everyday life."[13]

Culture is all about shared everyday, human experience. It is, as Stuart Hall notes, "*both* the meanings and values which arise amongst distinctive social groups and classes, on the basis of their given historical conditions and relationships, through which they 'handle' and respond to the conditions of existence; *and* as the lived traditions and practices through which those 'understandings' are expressed and in which they are embodied."[14]

Hall's definition of culture bears the implication of a second common trait of cultural studies. His acknowledgment of the distinctive nature of social groups and classes begs the follow-up point about the inevitability of tension between them, for "no 'whole way of life' is without its dimension of struggle and confrontation between opposed *ways* of life."[15] Distinctive cultural identity presumes distinctive, and very often contrasting, cultural belief. When those identities and beliefs harden, as they always do, into social and political positions, we have entered the realm of ideology. Cultural studies' natural interest in the relationship between such cultures means that it is at its most basic level invested in the matter of ideological criticism. Storey concludes: "Ideology is without doubt the central concept in cultural studies."[16]

Many scholars connect this emphasis on ideology to the early influence of Marxism on the development of cultural studies as a discipline. Even scholars who have disputed the level of Marxism's influence and pointed out the reasons why cultural studies moved beyond its limited scope recognize its initial contributions.[17] They were primarily two. First, cultural studies argues that culture must always be studied in relationship to the place it occupies in history. Culture is an incarnational phenomenon, inscribed in history, valued by history, coexistent with history, and in turn pressing the case of its own interests and identity onto history. While the earlier cultural studies interpreters wanted to lock that incarnational moment into the Marxist framework of production and consumption, later analysts recognized a broader historical scope and allowed their study of culture to broaden with it. It is a case of not just reading a text against its historical background, but also seeing history and text inscribed in each other.[18] Second, as Storey points out,

> cultural studies assumes that capitalist industrial societies are societies divided unequally along ethnic, gender, generational and class lines. It contends that culture is one of the principal sites where this division is established and contested: culture is a terrain on which takes place a continual struggle over meaning, in which subordinate groups attempt to resist the imposition of meanings which bear the interests of dominant groups. It is this which makes culture ideological.[19]

It is this interest that drives the investment of cultural studies in ideological criticism.

When directing this ideological lens onto the study of culture, the cultural studies researcher emphasizes that her investment is in *contemporary* culture. She is quite distinct from the characteristic biblical interpreter, who seeks primarily to situate the text within and interpret its meaning in light of its past, ancient context. The cultural studies interpreter wants to know how contemporary cultures interact with each other and with texts and, more to my own investigative point, how contemporary cultures invest themselves, their agendas, their interests, and their presuppositions into their reading process. The goal is not to determine what Revelation meant in John's first-century community; the goal is to ascertain how material written in and for that community becomes meaningful for a particular twenty-first-century community.

Such an ambition mandates a multidisciplinary approach. One cannot comprehend how texts become meaningful for contemporary communities by appealing exclusively to analyses of historical contexts and/or literary clues. While necessary, those methodologies are by themselves insufficient. The cultural studies researcher prides herself on being malleable and reactive, able to adjust to the investigative circumstances with disciplines that meet specific, current needs. No wonder McRobbie contends that "cultural studies must continue to argue against its incorporation into what is conventionally recognized as a 'subject area.' For cultural studies to survive it cannot afford to lose this disciplinary looseness, this feeling that, like other radical areas of inquiry, . . . its authors are making it up as they go along."[20]

Cultural studies labels and celebrates these "loose" authors as organic intellectuals. According to Stephen Moore and Hall, the organic intellectual works on two fronts. "First of all, he or she must be on the cutting edge of intellectual work."[21] A multidisciplinary approach ideologically focused on contemporary communities and the way they build meaning as they interact with texts suggests exactly that. But there is a second component that democratizes the process of intellectual pursuit. The organic intellectual refuses to target his work only to other intellectuals. This researcher "cannot absolve himself or herself from the responsibility of transmitting those ideas, that knowledge, through the intellectual function, to those who do not belong, professionally, in the intellectual class."[22] The organic intellectual not only teaches; he teaches broadly, to a popular as well as a scholarly audience.

This study of common, ideological, contemporary ways of life via a multidisciplinary strategy deployed by intellectuals seeking to instruct and influence broad, popular audiences implies a political agenda. Indeed, the literary foundation of cultural studies—the idea that texts have meaning potential that is accessed contextually—is a political seedbed. John Storey points to the influence of Soviet linguist and philosopher Valentin Volosinov. "Volosinov argues that meaning is determined by the social context in which it is articulated. Cultural texts and practices are 'multiaccentual'; that is, they can be articulated with different 'accents' by different people in different contexts for different politics."[23] Different communities access the meaning potential of texts to different ends because of the way they "culturally" read those texts. This suggests not only that their politics will determine their reading; it ensures that their "political" readings will come into contact and very often into conflict with the readings of other, differently situated communities. The interaction between those communities, as each one jockeys to position its reading in a more authoritative light, is inevitably a political one.[24]

The cultural studies interpreter doesn't merely sit on the sidelines and record this struggle; she participates in it. This is what Grossberg, Nelson, and Treichler mean when they say that "in virtually all traditions of cultural studies, its practitioners see cultural studies not simply as a chronicle of cultural change but as an intervention in it, and see themselves not simply as scholars providing an account but as politically engaged participants."[25] They call this engagement "making a difference." How so? As McRobbie points out,

> Theoretical developments combine with a sense of political urgency bringing to cultural studies what we might still expect of it, a mode of study which is engaged and which seeks not the truth, but knowledge and understanding as a practical and material means of communicating with and helping to empower subordinate social groups and movements.[26]

The cultural studies interpreter not only recognizes that all readings are culturally and therefore politically contrived; she also realizes that all readings are politically situated. That is to say, the readings of texts made by communities of greater power tend to be more highly authorized than the readings made by communities of lesser power. The cultural studies reader tries to level the interpretive playing field not only by pointing out that all readings are culturally located and therefore on that basis "equal"; she also presses the cause of the reading made by the less empowered community to ensure that it has a proper hearing as an effective and meaningful way of reading text. This is precisely the effort I will want to make with regard to an African American reading of John's Apocalypse.

Cultural Studies: An Introduction

Before examining how a cultural studies model can be particularly helpful for an African American reading of the Apocalypse, it is useful to chart the course of development of this "methodology." In reviewing its history, readers will be able to determine precisely *how* its character traits came into place, and *why* as a "method" of study it is uniquely suited to the kind of work I propose in my effort to reveal Revelation's intent for contemporary Christian discipleship. I see two key phases; I label them "Genesis" and "Exodus."

Genesis

Cultural studies' genesis begins with the "Culture and Civilization" work of Matthew Arnold and F. R. Leavis. As described by Ralph Broadbent, Arnold was a powerful educator who held a significant government position in England. An elitist, when he talked of culture, he meant the "high" culture of the arts, sciences, and sophisticated society, the kind "well exemplified by ancient Athens."[27] The adjective *best* most appropriately defined the kind of culture Arnold intended: the ability to know what is best; the mental and spiritual application of what is best; the pursuit of what is best. And who could best decide what was best and how it should best be established in society? Who else but the best of society, the cultural elite?[28] It is all very political. One not only enjoyed the best; one pursued it, and one hoped to transform society in the light of it. How would this happen? According to Arnold's strategic design, the middle class could be trained in the ways of classic English literature. Its members would subsequently become the cultural elite that was competent to rule. As Broadbent points out "English literature, and especially poetry, can change the middle class from its narrowness and fit it to govern. It can also hold society (and empire) together and contain the real danger of anarchy represented by the working class."[29]

Picking up where Arnold left off, Leavis, a literary critic, also championed the cultural power of English literature. For him "the problem was 'dumbing down.' This mass culture was seen as a threat to 'proper' culture and frightened those around [him]."[30] Equally concerned that one define culture in politically transformative ways, he envisioned a corps of "cultural missionaries" who could, operating from their educational base camps, instruct students in the opposition of "mass" culture. The objective was clear: do not allow anything of contemporary culture, that is, the non-classics, to have any kind of interpretive sway in life. The only appropriate interpretive norm was orthodox, classical culture.[31]

In biblical studies, a similar principle holds sway. Here, of course, historical and literary criticism operate as the classical norms against which all other forms of biblical interpretation are judged and found wanting. Just as mass culture was a danger to the literary norms of Arnold and Leavis, the contemporary and mass contexts of culturally located and influenced readers are a threat to the methodological purity and clarity of biblical criticism. The difference is that Leavis and Arnold were honest; they acknowledged that culture as they understood it was openly and aggressively ideological. In fact, they celebrated its ideology; high culture's very goal was the transformation of society to the point that every element of society operated from its enlightened perspective. Historical and literary biblical criticism have also had their methodological missionary movements. While their adherents have taught and celebrated their "high" research strategies, they have warned against contemporary "cultural readings" and the interpretive "dumbing down" that goes along with them. Yet

many of their proponents persist in a dogged refusal to acknowledge their own corresponding, interpretive ideology and the
political agenda of dominance that goes along with it.

Arnold and Leavis certainly would not have been amused with
the kind of culturally oriented reading of Revelation that I propose. No doubt, the African American lens I propose to use would
cut against the grain of what they considered "high culture." And
yet their work does allow for the kind of interpretive strategy that
recognizes the ideological nature of all interpretation and celebrates that reality and its transformative intent. It is that celebration and intent that I wish to carry forward. I find my precedent
in the work of cultural studies.

Exodus

Cultural studies began as a direct challenge to the elitist and aristocratic "Culture and Civilization" movement. Disgusted with the
view that high culture, trained into an educated elite, should
trickle down in various forms of intellectual and social patronage
to the lower classes, scholars such as Richard Hoggart, Raymond
Williams, and E. P. Thompson stretched the meaning of culture
and thereby opened up the study of it.[32] By starting from the definition of culture as a "whole way of life," these scholars established the possibility of bringing contemporary popular culture
into the investigative enterprise. Cheryl Exum and Moore quote
Williams:

> The analysis of culture, from such a definition . . . will . . .
> include analysis of elements . . . that to followers of other def-
> initions are not "culture" at all: the organization of produc-
> tion, the structure of the family, the structure of institutions
> which express or govern social relationships, the character-
> istic forms through which members of the society commu-
> nicate.[33]

The eventual scope proved to be massive. According to Moore,
by the mid-1990s, "cultural studies had expanded its maw to swal-

low popular culture whole and entire, all the way from Disney to pornography."[34]

The politics was clearly one of empowerment; its instigation came from the very cultural circumstances of the cultural studies thinkers who thought it up. Though scholars, they were not themselves representatives of the high culture that Arnold and Leavis so admired and so wished to expand. Williams and Hoggart were from working-class families. Once they'd gained entrance into the institutions of British higher education, they initiated a kind of educational subversion. Instead of evangelizing others into the high culture into which they had themselves been admitted, they redefined culture and studied it wherever they found it, and they found it in the social contexts out of which they themselves had come. In fact, Nelson, Grossberg, and Treichler argue that "their need to make their own cultural heritage part of the culture universities study and remember helped motivate some of their early publications."[35] Equally impressive, they began by sharing what they learned not in ivory towers, but in the broadest and most "popular" of public realms. The majority of them had begun their teaching careers not in universities, but in adult education programs.

Richard Hoggart pioneered the movement. His book, *The Uses of Literacy: Aspects of Working-Class Life, with Special Reference to Publications and Entertainment*, in 1957 helped provide a critical foundation. Moore declares that his study of working-class culture and popular media anticipated what cultural studies would one day become.[36] Hoggart was, however, somewhat reticent in his boundary-crossing effort. While his work on the working class challenged the high-culture politics of Arnold and Leavis, he did not make the full move toward an acceptance of what he called "mass," popular culture. Mass culture, he believed, caused passivity and created a false sense of group feeling and conformity that might very well prove destabilizing and destructive for the working-class culture he championed.[37] Real community existed in the active living out of working-class culture, not in some publicized approximation of community that existed only in media images and popular belief.

Like Hoggart, Raymond Williams included the culture of the working class in his studies. He, however, went farther. In his two books, *Culture and Society* (1958) and *The Long Revolution* (1961), he made the critical redefinition of culture to include a "whole way of life." The implications were astounding; Exum and Moore speak of the effect as a paradigm shift.[38] Broadbent states the case well: "The point Williams is making is that language and literature cannot help but be affected by wider society. There is no ideologically pure 'English' and meaning is socially constructed."[39] In the case of biblical studies, this means that meaning is revealed in the interaction between a text and an interpreter as he or she stands located within the life of a particular, contemporary community. What is determined to be meaningful about that text is that part of the text's meaning potential that corresponds informatively with the interpreter's cultural location and perspective. In other words, where meaning is concerned, it is culture, even mass, contemporary culture, that reveals.

E. P. Thompson entered the debate with his 1963 book, *The Making of the English Working Class*. Strikingly political in intent, Thompson's work has been labeled by a multitude of scholars as an example of cultural history "written from below."[40] Instead of commending and continuing the practice of writing history from the experience of "kings and queens," Thompson challenged that "history, without the experience (in the widest sense) of 'ordinary' men and women, is not history but some form of ideology."[41] But that is precisely the case with much of historical writing and particularly, at least throughout most of its existence, the writing in the field of biblical studies. Broadbent argues the case by appealing to British commentaries on the New Testament. He wants to determine whether they have been written in such a way that the voices of those from the margins, "from below," have been written out of the discussion. The answer he finds is not surprising. In appealing, for example, to the British commentaries on Romans 13:1–7, he finds a very passive and conservative acceptance of the need for citizens to acquiesce to the role of the state. In reading the Synoptic text where Jesus discusses the payment of taxes to Caesar, he points to commentaries that recognized the coin to be symbolic of Roman "slavery." Yet those commentaries still maintained that compliance with that authoritarian state was the will of God expressed in the text. Henry Barclay's Mark commentary provides illustrative testimony: "Granted that payment was a badge of slavery, there are circumstances, Christ teaches, under which slavery must be borne."[42] Need one really wonder whether a slave's reading "from below" might possibly yield a contrary conclusion? The extreme case of enslavement need not be invoked; even the difficulties of impoverishment were ignored. "No mention is made in any of the commentaries, including more recent ones such as Hooker's (1991) of the immense difficulties involved for those who had to pay the taxes."[43]

R. S. Sugirtharajah makes a similar case regarding British commentaries written "for" Indian Christians. Operating from a focus on Christian morality and mission that mandated a strong critique of Indian "superstition and immorality," these commentaries created a worldview that endorsed the ethics and principles of British Christianity. They simultaneously condemned all indigenous Indian beliefs and practices. Any proposal for interpreting Christian texts through Indian culture could therefore be summarily dismissed.

While Bengalis like Rammohun Roy, Keshub Chunder Sen, and Pratap Chunder Moozumdar, all members of the Brahmo Samaj, a Hindu reform movement, tried to rescue Jesus from denominational, doctrinal, and colonial entanglement, and recast him as an Asiatic figure, these [English] commentaries warn their readers of the folly of such attempts at indigenization.[44] Once again the political implications were potent. "The effect of all this is to establish British dominance and to provide the moral imperative for imperial intervention, subjugation and the prolongation of the British presence in a heathen land."[45]

Cultural studies fights back against this. It recognizes the intent of historical and literary critical methods to dismiss readings "from below," to appeal instead to "objective" methodologies that valorize the dominant cultural ideology inscribed within them, while all the time arguing that no such ideology exists. Cultural studies is different. As Broadbent recognizes, "it draws attention to local or popular sub-cultures. Should we not also be studying popular works on the Bible? Examples might include Bible reading notes,

Bible videos, children's Bibles, Christian rock music—the list is endless. It may be this type of study that reveals voices resistant to the dominant tradition."[46]

It is precisely this type of study that I want to pursue in my reading of Revelation "from below." In analyzing the language of Revelation from the perspective of the subculture of the African American church, I will need to look through a variety of "subcultural," indigenous material. As there are extremely few African American biblical scholars, there will not be a great many African American commentaries on the text. The use of popular material such as sermons and hymns therefore becomes critical. According to the foundational principles of cultural studies, their use is essential if an interpretative strategy is to reveal the meaning of the text from and for the African American culture I have in mind.

The groundbreaking work of Hoggart, Williams, and Thompson was championed at the Centre for Contemporary Cultural Studies (CCCS) in Birmingham, England. Established in 1964 as a graduate annex of the English department at the University of Birmingham, the Centre provided a haven for scholars who not only wanted to study mass and popular culture, but also wanted to use the results of that study as a lens through which they might analyze societal products like biblical literature. The earliest theoretical influence on the efforts of those who populated the Centre was the work of Louis Althusser. Althusser's work is credited with giving cultural studies its trademark emphasis on ideology.

Briefly put, Althusser established a system of analyzing culture that concentrated interest on the behavior of autonomous and yet interlocking social institutions like churches, schools, and families. These *social* institutions were different from the apparatuses devised by the state (government, army, police, courts, etc.). State institutions mandate expected behavior by force. "By *covertly* inducing people to behave in socially acceptable ways, [these interlocking social institutions] do the subtle work of ideology."[47] By concentrating on these institutions, cultural studies focused more and more on the ideological presumptions that drove them. No wonder, then, that Exum and Moore can claim that "Althusser's enduring legacy to British cultural studies . . . has consisted in inducing it to make ideology . . . a central focus of attention."[48]

Moore points to another signal moment in the life of the Centre in the late 1970s, when work produced there assumed a positive view of popular culture generally and youth subculture specifically. Hoggart's resistance to the study of popular culture had not only been broken through; it had been completely overturned. In fact, it was through the various forms in which popular culture took shape, his successors now realized, that cultures "from below" promulgated their ideological positions and interests. As Moore more cogently puts it, "The theme of ideological resistance [is] expressed through subcultural style."[49]

The feminist movement of the 1970s is a magnificent subcultural example of one such resistance movement. Ironically, its work at the Centre began as an ideological critique of cultural studies. It not only wanted to use the methodological assumptions of cultural studies; it targeted the transformation of cultural studies' androcentric ideology as one of its primary investigative and political objectives. Stuart Hall, the second director of the Centre, is candid: "As a thief in the night, [feminism] broke in: interrupted, made an unseemly noise, seized the time, crapped on the table of cultural studies."[50] Focused on matters of gender and sexuality, the feminist scholars at the Centre were keenly critical of their academic brothers' inability or lack of desire to critique the sexism and misogyny of many of the youth subcultures or popular media genres they otherwise so assiduously studied.[51]

The matter of race and ethnicity had a similarly critical impact; Hall referred to it as the "second interruption."[52] While writing in 1992, Paul Gilroy could sound out his pleasure that "ethnicity has been mobilized as part of [cultural studies'] distinctive hermeneutic."[53] Hall, however, allows that early on only a profound struggle forced the matter of race onto the agenda. A racial/ethnic scholar of Jamaican heritage himself, Hall was perhaps uniquely positioned to initiate and successfully prosecute this struggle. From Hoggart's departure in 1968 until 1979, the period that Moore calls "the Golden Age of British Cultural Studies," he was the director of the CCCS. Convinced that religion is an ideological domain, he pursued the manner in which religion functioned ideologically in his native Jamaica.[54] Working descriptively, he chronicled the era of plantation slavery in Jamaica and demonstrated how ideological resistance develops through the particular subcultural style of Jamaican Christianity. "Christianity inadvertently provided an officially sanctioned space in which slaves could assemble publicly and learn potentially subversive skills such as reading, even if only to read the Bible."[55]

Hall's work with Jamaican Rastafarianism is perhaps even more ideologically illuminating. He demonstrates how the disciples of Marcus Garvey developed the doctrines of Ras Tafari from the Bible through the metaphorical connection they drew between the Ethiopian emperor Haile Selassie I and the biblical Lion of Judah. How did this small religious sect then become a "mass-cultural ideology," "an indigenous Jamaican expression of black nationalism?"[56] Moore shares how it saturated society with its ideology not through churches or missionaries, but through reggae music that was "littered with biblical and rasta references."[57] And from Jamaica, principally via its music, it spread to the black ghettos of British cities like Birmingham. Operating from a unique, island subcultural experience, the export created, in the process of encounter with a new culture in a new land, another distinctive resistance subculture an ocean away. According to Hall, the black counterculture that emerged provided "the basis of new modes of self-discovery and self-identity for blacks, as well as ethnic pride, a sense of history and culture, ways of articulating the experience of oppression and forms in which to imagine an alternative future."[58]

Hall's work demonstrated how an alternative reading of the Bible led to a changed view about the working of the world. In the process, both in Jamaica and England, these believers were able to value positively their own popular culture and simultaneously resist the cultures that denigrated them. The process of consciously rereading the Bible through their cultural lens reshaped their very cultural landscape. A new Bible effected a new existence, an existence of self-affirmation and political resistance. One wonders if a self-conscious reading of the apocalyptic language and expectations for discipleship in the book of Revelation through an African American lens might yield a similar result.

Fernando Segovia and Cultural Studies: Reading from This Place

The work of Fernando Segovia suggests that it can. According to Moore, Segovia is the first biblical scholar to apply the term cultural studies to his work.[59] One of his articles in the landmark volumes *Reading from This Place* is entitled "Cultural Studies and Contemporary Biblical Criticism: Ideological Criticism as Mode of Discourse."[60]

To be sure, "the process of painstakingly 'translating' extrabiblical cultural studies into a biblical studies idiom is not one that interests Segovia."[61] His work, however, clearly builds from the legacy established by Hoggart, Williams, Thompson, Hall, and the CCCS. For one thing, Segovia presses the point of ideology. His own brand of ideological criticism challenges the manner in which classical biblical criticism, perpetuated in the "high" culture of historical and literary analysis, assumed a kind of methodological pride of place. The positivistic assumption that the historical or literary critic, by virtue of an appeal to a method of criticism itself, could inoculate himself from the influence of his cultural location, and therefore cultural perspective, was challenged and denied outright. Segovia was convinced that every reading was a reading from a particular place and, moreover, that such readings were inscribed with the ideologies invested in those places. Those readings were therefore very much political mechanisms designed to champion a particular reading strategy *and* the meaning it constructed.

For a second, related thing, Segovia understands the importance of the flesh-and-blood, culturally located, ideologically influenced reader. For him the reader is not an academic construct or a scholarly paradigm; she is a flesh-and-blood entity caught up in and given life and identity by a particular cultural location. This flesh-and-blood reader does not "find" objective meaning in the text the way a dog digs up a bone in the backyard; she participates in the construction of meaning as she places her entire cultural self in the kind of constructive engagement with a text that can be described only as a living encounter. "Meaning emerges, therefore, as a result of an encounter between a socially and historically conditioned text and a socially and historically conditioned reader."[62] It is no wonder, then, that when she reads the text she learns something about herself as well as the text, and when she applies the text it changes not only her reading, but also her very life.

How does this biblical movement from historical and literary criticism to cultural studies take shape? Segovia's work implies a certain inevitability. He attributes this to the inexorable demand that previously silenced communities "from below" make for text readings that value their flesh-and-blood life realities. It would not be unlike the pressure feminists and racial ethnics exerted on cultural studies itself, even as it was exerting the pressure of working-class, mass, and popular cultural ways of life on classical views of culture and cultural study. One might capture the sense of this inevitability by paraphrasing the saying Martin Luther King Jr. made famous during the height of the African American civil rights movement: though the arc of history is long, its bend is ultimately toward justice. Segovia's claim appears to correspond: though the arc of interpretive biblical history is long, its bend is ultimately in the direction of a liberating, decolonizing cultural approach to biblical reading.

Segovia charts the movement by categorizing the history of biblical research into four primary paradigms.[63] In the first paradigm, *historical* criticism, the biblical text was seen as the means to the historical world out of which the author rose. The key emphasis was always on a text's social location. The intent was to ascertain how the text came to meaning in the original context for which it was written. That was the one meaning that was universally applicable across time and space. In the second paradigm, *literary* criticism, the emphasis was on the text as medium. Instead of focusing on the world "behind the text," the literary critic was mesmerized by the aesthetic quality of the text as literature. The two different criticisms did, however, share a common trait: "the meaning of the text still tended to be regarded as univocal and objective and hence as retrievable on the basis of a rigorous application of proper and scientific methodology."[64]

It was not the press of flesh-and-blood readers "from below" that initially challenged this view that a single, objective meaning could be extracted from a text. The implications of literary criticism did that. Language critics acknowledged the polysemic nature of all linguistic signs. This recognition gave "rise to the concept of a plurality of interpretations based on the text itself; no interpretation, it was now argued, could exhaust the meaning of a text."[65] Even though for Segovia this was a push in the right direction, he realized that literary criticism was unable to move far enough. "In the end, however, the principle of a plurality of interpretations was always fairly circumscribed, with a view of such interpretations as ultimately subject to the constraints imposed by the text."[66] In other words, though the linguistic markings did have a great deal of meaning potential, those markings themselves somehow told readers, even those from radically different cultures, which part of the meaning potential was to be accessed as the only "acceptable" meaning.

In the third paradigm, what Segovia describes as *cultural* criticism, the text was understood to be both the means and the medium. The emphasis was one of reading the text in light of its original historical context, then making use of various social science models to elucidate that context and the text itself. This methodology, too, promised an access to *the* objective and universally correct text meaning.

In the fourth paradigm, *cultural studies*, researchers shifted in a new direction. For the cultural studies reader the text is neither means nor medium; it is a construction that takes shape when an ideologically positioned reader, with or without an equally positioned methodology, engages the meaning potential of the text. Because this reader is always ideologically situated, the meaning she constructs from that potential will always be ideologically conditioned. The end result is a democratization of the interpretative process. Because no reading can claim to be disinterested and therefore objective, every reading engages every other reading on equal ground. This is what Segovia refers to as the liberating, decolonizing effect of cultural studies. "Such a reading calls for a 'speaking in other tongues,' in one's own tongue. . . . Such a reading also calls for critical dialogue among the many tongues."[67] It is the only kind of reading that, instead of seeking to establish itself above all other readings as the one correct interpretation, "looks for a truly global interaction" among many variously situated, ideologically vested, flesh-and-blood readings.

It is this "global interaction," this sometimes tense grinding of one positioned interpretation against another, that prevents communities with political intentions that are hostile to the well-being of neighboring communities from running illegitimately away with text meaning. As Segovia himself puts it:

> It should be pointed out in this regard that the critical situation envisioned is not necessarily one where "anything goes," since readers and interpreters are always positioned and interested and thus always engaged in evaluation and construction: both texts and "texts" are constantly analyzed and engaged, with acceptance or rejection, full or partial, as ever-present and ever-shifting possibilities.[68]

In other words, there is a difference between a reading from this place and a reading that runs indiscriminately all over the place. The check, however, does not come from some arbitrarily established, universal meaning standard; it arises instead out of the check and balance of communities equally involved with the text and equally vested with the interpretive authority to engage the text's meaning potential from their cultural place in life.

A political force, this kind of cultural reading compels change. Segovia and others describe the new reality it encourages and helps establish as postcolonial biblical reading. The conclusions reached by dominant cultures and the historical, literary, and social scientific methods they deployed no longer rule the interpretive domain. When the voices of cultures "from below" take themselves seriously enough to propel themselves into the exegetical, hermeneutical, and interpretive debate, the imperium claimed and held by dominant cultures is broken. It is not just a new reading of the Bible that emerges as a result; a new Bible emerges, just as it did in the Rastafarian community analyzed by Hall. Surely, this is what Exum and Moore mean when they write that "Biblical Studies/Cultural Studies is not just the Bible influencing culture or culture reappropriating the Bible, but a process of unceasing mutual redefinition in which cultural appropriations constantly reinvent the Bible, which in turn constantly impels new appropriations."[69]

How will it happen? How will the identity of the Bible itself shift in the process? As he presses the case, the cultural reader will come to realize that not only does he *read* the biblical materials from his particular twenty-first-century cultural location; he will come to fully appreciate the fact that the texts themselves were *written* in and from particular first-century contexts. Those texts are therefore as inscribed with the ideologies of those first-century cultures as his twenty-first-century readings are vested with his own culture's ideological positions. This recognition doesn't simply change the way he reads and interprets the Bible; it transforms the very Bible he interprets. Only when the colonialism in the text itself is thereby acknowledged and laid bare can one begin to search within the text for those first-century voices "from below" that are struggling to make themselves an accessible part of the text's meaning potential. Sugirtharajah is succinct:

> [Postcolonial criticism] will reconsider the biblical narratives as emanating from colonial contexts. It will revalue the colonial ideology, stigmatization and negative portrayals embedded in the content, plot and characterization. It will scour the biblical pages for how colonial intentions and assumptions informed the production of the texts. . . . It will attempt to resurrect lost voices and causes which are distorted or silenced in the canonized text.[70]

This is how cultural biblical studies operates politically as postcolonial biblical studies. It begins by valuing the interpretive conclusions of previously marginalized contemporary communities; its ends up giving an ear to the marginalized voices struggling for sound within the texts themselves. It begins by challenging the way we read the Bible; it ends up challenging the very Bible the "higher" criticisms have taught us to read.

A Test Case: Reading Revelation from Particular Places

Although Tina Pippin and Catherine Keller do not lay specific claim to the title "cultural studies," both operate according to principles that fit Segovia's understanding of cultural biblical studies. As feminists, they are reading Revelation "from below," with the political intent to transform the way in which the larger critical community sees and evaluates its canonical language.

Right from the start Pippin sounds the part of a researcher dedicated to the principles of cultural studies. She admits that for her "the starting point is a literary reading that focuses on the political and ethical dimensions of the text, known as ideology critique. Ideology critique is based on the idea that texts are produced (and continue to be produced) in political 'contexts.'"[71] She also knows that texts are engaged from political contexts; she acknowledges that this is what she intentionally sets out to do: "I want to reveal my ideological biases in reading the Apocalypse. My reading is based on certain political and ethical presuppositions regarding the Apocalypse."[72] She recognizes that the text has a great deal of meaning potential; she knows that her political and ethical positioning will play a huge role in helping her determine what part of that potential she will access as meaningful. "Multiple readings of the Apocalypse," she goes on to say, "are possible and indeed necessary. I offer only one of many possible readings of the Apocalypse—only one possible way to push the boundaries of reading."[73] And she realizes finally the political power inherent in texts and the interpretations of them. "In other words," she presses, "texts that are given authority in a community affect people's lives. I am interested in the ways the Apocalypse influences women's (and men's) lives."[74]

To determine that influence, Pippin initiates what she calls a "gynocritical" reading that lays bare the author's focus on the desire for and the death of the female.[75] "Reading the text as a woman demands reading for the gender codes in the narrative where women appear or are noticeably absent. The archetypes of women (virgin and whore) show the displacement of women in the text."[76] Revelation's ethical universe requires the reader to make an either/or decision between the Lamb and the Beast. Pippin argues that the characterization of women in the narrative has been manipulated so as to make the reader's ability to walk the path to the right decision for the Lamb dependent upon his willingness to visualize women as anarchic threats whose identities must be either controlled or destroyed. Having deciphered this colonial hostility towards women in the text, she subsequently pursues the colonial strategies that have dominated interpretation of the text for centuries.

According to Pippin, in Revelation's ethical universe the ultimate goal is revolution. The ruling power, symbolized most graphically by the female metaphor "whore of Babylon," will be killed and eaten in a macabre, eschatological feast. This death (along with Jezebel's) is the female death that the book so desperately covets. There is yet another female, however, who is deeply desired. She is the new Jerusalem, adorned as a bride for her husband, penetrated by the 144,000 males who have remained steadfast and faithful in their witness to the lordship of Christ. This new Jerusalem is a desirable female body, as is the woman clothed with the sun from chapter 12. Pippin points out that neither of them, however, is given an active role of transformation in the story. They remain desirable objects, not active subjects. And their power, their sensuality, is kept in check by their role as either busy breeder (the woman clothed with the sun) or blushing bride. Her conclusion: "The making of archetypes of the female and the abuse of women's bodies reveal a deep misogyny."[77]

Pippin recognizes that there are feminist writers (Elisabeth Schüssler Fiorenza; Adela Yarbro Collins) who try to transcend this misogynistic language and provide positive readings of the book. In that sense, she allows that there is sufficient meaning potential for readings that are more favorable than her own. She even concedes that some perspectives, like those of persons living in the two-thirds world, in the midst of war, or destroyed by some great oppression, could access that potential in ways that would create a legitimate decolonizing reading of Revelation. "A political reading using liberation theology does reveal the call to endurance and hope in the text, and this reading is important."[78] Through this lens the expectation for Revelation-style discipleship is clear: active, nonviolent resistance.[79] In the end, though, none of that can overwhelm the hostility she finds inscribed in the book when she reads it gynocritically. Simply put, "the Apocalypse is not liberating for women readers."[80]

Catherine Keller need not even wait for an actual reading of the text before making a critical assessment; the title John chooses, Apocalypse, reveals the patriarchy and the sexism right at the start. Pointing out that the prebiblical connotation of the term is the "marital stripping of the veiled virgin," she reminds her readers that "the revealing [stripping] gaze is male."[81] Because Pippin's work already so carefully accesses that part of the meaning potential that is hostile toward women, it is useful in looking at Keller to move directly to her concern about the book's violence. She is immensely concerned about the binary nature of the Apocalypse and, indeed, apocalyptic literature in general. Apocalyptic literature crafts a world of clear-cut either-ors. One is either good or bad. It is instructive that some of John's harshest remarks to any of his seven churches concern the one community that refused to be either hot or cold but tried to find a way to sit lukewarmly in between. Ethically this means that decisions must be made to fight for the good and fight against the bad. Since the bad *is* bad, one must fight it until it is utterly destroyed. For Keller, feminism demands "a de-dramatization of the 'fight to the death' between rival groups and thus between the sexes."[82] This is particularly important since in most cases, as in Revelation as Pippin has pointed out, the good tends to be symbolized in male imagery while the bad tends toward the feminine metaphor.[83]

Keller is very concerned about the ethics that follows from this kind of either-or approach. It tends to promote one of two types of responses to evil in the world, neither of which is particularly helpful. The first response is an urgent messianism that seeks complete and total transformation as the only acceptable outcome. The second is a radical passivity that surrenders in the face of evil, because only God represents a good powerful enough to overcome it.

Recognizing, as did Pippin, the liberative and transformative potential in Revelation's language, Keller also sees positive possibilities. But in this case, as might any cultural studies reader, she promotes a rereading of the text from her political, feminist perspective. In this case, she suggests we read Revelation from the space of what she terms a counterapocalypse. Why? Because the counterapocalypse uses the strengths of apocalyptic (its urgency, its transformative potential) as the very means of overcoming its weaknesses (its misogyny, its violence, its binary dualism). And so she concludes: "If, then, counter-apocalypse echoes and parodies apocalypse in order to disarm its polarities, it also savors its intensity, its drive for justice, its courage in the face of impossible odds and losses."[84]

Pippin and Keller are good test cases because they are consciously reading from acknowledged ideological spaces. They recognize the political import of their readings, and they know precisely what kinds of transformations they hope their readings will inspire. At the same time, they recognize that they are accessing only selected portions of the book's overall meaning potential. They acknowledge that others may well read differently; it is this acknowledgment that enables me to demonstrate precisely how other readers, reading from different cultural spaces, engage their readings and suggest the valuation of different parts of Revelation's meaning potential.

Pippin had already mentioned the readings of Fiorenza and Collins as alternative feminist appraisals on the value of Revelation for women readers. The work of David Barr is different not only because this self-described "feminist reader" is a male, but, perhaps more importantly, because he reads no need to "transcend" the language in order to make it useful for women disciples. Barr recognizes that methodologies, too, are invested with their ideological perspective and the choice of methodology can make a big difference in how one accesses a text's meaning potential. His narrative approach enables a particular kind of meaning access.[85] "A narrative reading of John's Apocalypse will allow us to see new ways to address both the issue of coercion and domination by power and the issue of God's failure to act to end innocent suffering in the interim."[86] In other words, one need not read against the text or stop reading the text altogether; one can read from the text the kind of ethical direction that transforms the world positively for everyone. Apparently, it is the unique combination of Barr's narrative methodology, his feminist concern, and his male identity that makes this reading as possible for him as it was impossible for Pippin and Keller.

Reading John's work narratively, Barr fixates on the image of the conquering Lamb (5:5–6). The transformative force in Revelation is revealed in the Lamb's weakness—calculated, aggressive, resistant weakness. Even though John represents Jesus in three different characterizations throughout his work—a majestic, humanlike figure (Rev. 1–3), a slaughtered, still standing Lamb (Rev. 4–11), and a heavenly warrior (Rev. 12–22)—Barr maintains that the central, dominating focus is always on the Lamb.[87] It is through the weakness of the Lamb that God's transformative will takes human and cosmic shape. "My point," he says, "is that this symbolic inversion is also a narrative inversion and that the narrative inversion is also a moral inversion: in the story evil only appears to be conquered by power. In this story, evil is conquered by the death of the lamb."[88]

Women, according to Barr, are also pictured in a much more nuanced way than Pippin would allow. The narrative language, he argues, depicts the woman whose death is desired, the whore, not as a woman, but a great city. He contends that "admitting this ambiguity changes the moral equation that comes from the Whore's destruction."[89] In other words, her destruction is perhaps more related to realities of state than gender. Barr believes this to be the case because of the positive imaging of women that Pippin's gynocritical review seems to miss. He points to the fact that "in each instance the evil woman is paired with an evil man: Jezebel/Balaam; Whore/Beast."[90] There are evil masculine characters (e.g., the dragon) opposed to good women characters (e.g., the woman clothed with the sun). And while Pippin finds that women are completely marginalized in Revelation, Barr argues that there is much more attention paid to the new Jerusalem as the bride than to the groom. "In fact," he goes on to say, "I find it striking that this community that can image itself as a covenant of celibate virgin males (14:4) can also image itself as a bride. In this story the male becomes the female, hardly a marginal image."[91] His conclusion, which challenges Pippin's final evaluation of the book, is a clear recognition that cultural location and the ideological presumptions that operate from it are clear and certain influences over text interpretation. "So I argue that John's story is not so misogynistic as Pippin suggests, that her deliberate reading 'as a woman' (53) too easily reifies negative feminine imagery and too easily overlooks positive feminine imagery."[92]

There is still the matter of the violence in the book, perpetuated by the binary (either-or) dualism. Evil must be eradicated by the good, whatever the cost. While Pippin, Keller, and Barr seem to agree that the disciples in Revelation are called to nonviolence (action or passivity), God clearly meets fire with apocalyptic fire. Barr argues that the violence is transcended in the book because God ultimately doesn't achieve victory through this retaliatory violence; instead, God's messianic agent wins by taking violence upon himself as the slaughtered Lamb. Even so, Barr knows there is a problem. "Still I regret the violence and wish the story were not so easy to read as accepting of violence."[93]

Is there a reading lens able to access even this meaning potential in a viably transformative way? Perhaps a place to start is with the work to which Pippin herself referred, Allan Boesak's Revelation commentary. Boesak knows not only that violence is practiced against God's people, but that God's people cry out for a matching recompense from the Lord (6:9–10). Boesak is clear that he isn't reading this text neutrally, but through the ideological perspective of a black South African enduring the oppressive weight of apartheid. The text's meaning is meaningful in and specifically for this particular way of life.

> At the moment of detention; in the long dark hours of incarceration; as the footsteps of your interrogators come down the passage to your cell; above the harsh voices and scornful

laugh; through the blows of fists on tender flesh, the blind-
ing pain of electric shocks; through the hazy, bloody mist of
unwanted tears; above the roar of guns and tanks and
armoured vehicles; in the nauseating sting of tear gas and the
tearing, searing burn of the bullet through your body—these
words are shouted, or whispered: "How long, Lord?"[94]

Boesak reads the call, and the attendant divine actions that go
along with it, as a call for and an acting out of necessary justice.
"People who do not know what oppression and suffering is react
strangely to the language of the Bible. The truth is that God *is* the
God of the poor and the oppressed. . . . Because they are power-
less, God will take up their cause and redeem them from oppression and violence. The oppressed do not see any dichotomy
between God's love and God's justice."[95] He seems impatient with
Christians who chastise John for not being more careful with his
language, more selective with his imagery, so that it would come
across as less violently oriented, so that its binary nature might be
toned down from harshness of moral black and white to the ambiguity of gray. Perhaps he even finds that such Christians stand
more on the immoral ground that must be overturned than on
the side of those who must overturn it. "Christians who enjoy
the fruits of injustice without a murmur, who remain silent as the
defenceless are slaughtered, dare not become indignant when the
suffering people of God echo the prayers of the psalms and pray
for deliverance and judgment."[96]

Miroslav Volf reads Revelation's violent language a decade
later, but does so out of a similarly haunted context, that of the
war-devastated Balkans (he is himself Croatian), and comes to a
similarly nuanced conclusion. For him, Rome reads as the pur-
veyor of a tyrannical system that threatens both human and cosmic life. It is a killer creature with a malevolent instinct to destroy
anything that fails to worship its nature and participate in its
political and economic exploitation. Does the rider on the white
horse, the Jesus image that preoccupies 19:11–21, respond to
horrors perpetuated by this beastly force with violence? Can it be

justified? From his reading angle, through his reading lens, apparently so:

> The violence of the Rider is the righteous judgment against this system of the one called "Faithful and True." (Revelation 19:11). Without such judgment there can be no world of peace, of truth, and of justice: terror (the "beast" that devours) and propaganda (the "false prophet" that deceives) must be overcome, evil must be separated from good, and darkness from light.[97]

If that sounds like the binary dualism that Keller wants to counter, your ears do not deceive you. Volf knows about the trust many place in the power of nonviolence and the belief that there is some spark of good in every power that pulls it toward proper response to that nonviolent call for transformative justice. Volf, though, isn't so sure. "In this belief," he writes, "one can smell a bit too much of the sweet aroma of a suburban ideology, entertained often by people who are neither courageous nor honest enough to reflect on the implications of terror taking place right in the middle of their living rooms!"[98] Too often, he grieves, nonviolence not only fails to break the grip of evil; its engagement with the powers of this earth often brings down horrific suffering upon the very heads of those who unleash it. In the worldview of Revelation, this is precisely the scenario he finds; there is no power great enough to stop the beasts from wanting to be beasts. In both John's world and our own, "this is where God's anger comes in."[99] That anger, he argues, is consistent with the sacrificial love God shows on the cross. And so we have what Volf calls a polarity within the heart of Christianity; a crucified Lamb who turns out to be the rider on the white horse. "After all, the cross is not forgiveness pure and simple, but God's *setting aright the world of injustice and deception.* The polarity is there because some human beings refuse to be 'set aright.'"[100] Can the Christian accept such a premise, endure such a polarity, and remain a disciple of a crucified Lord? Apparently so. "For the sake of the peace of God's good creation, we can and must affirm *this* divine anger and *this* divine violence, while at the same time holding on to the hope that in the end, even the flag bearer will desert the army that desires to make war against the Lamb."[101] Volf goes on to point out that Christians like Dietrich Bonhoeffer apparently came around to this way of thinking, and that even the pacifist Anabaptist tradition speaks without hesitation of God's wrath and judgment.[102]

While Volf in the end agrees that Revelation does not depict believers acting violently, he, like Boesak, seems to harbor little patience for Christians who upbraid John's chronicling of what he sees as God's necessary acts of judgment and justice. "They deem the talk of God's judgment irreverent . . . crude. And so violence thrives, secretly nourished by belief in a God who refuses to wield the sword."[103] While Christians follow the standard and act out the legacy of the crucified Messiah, they must, he argues, simultaneously recognize the right and need of the rider on the white horse to do what he needs to do. The ones who refute such a position have not seen as Volf himself has seen, do not read as Volf himself reads, through the cultural lens of a people who have been raped and pillaged by the bestial power of a force like the one John fights against in Rome.

> To the person who is inclined to dismiss [this thesis], I suggest imagining that you are delivering a lecture in a war zone (which is where a paper that underlies this chapter was originally delivered). Among your listeners are people whose cities and villages have been first plundered, then burned and leveled to the ground, whose daughters and sisters have been raped, whose fathers and brothers have had their throats slit. The topic of the lecture: a Christian attitude toward violence. The thesis: we should not retaliate since God is perfect noncoercive love. Soon you would discover that it takes the quiet of a suburban home for the birth of the thesis that human nonviolence corresponds to God's refusal to judge. In a scorched land, soaked in the blood of the innocent, it will invariably die. And as one watches it die, one will

do well to reflect about many other pleasant captivities of the liberal mind.[104]

Culture Reveals

How does one adjudicate between the different positions offered by Pippin and Keller, Barr, Boesak and Volf? Is one right and the others wrong? Are portions of one of their arguments mostly accurate, while argumentative portions of the others mostly inaccurate? And what would be the deciding factor in one or more of their favors? The historical critic would point to the milieu in which the text was originally constructed and argue for the interpretation whose conclusions made the most sense in that context. Cultural studies shows us, however, that the reconstruction of that milieu is itself radically influenced by the cultural location of the historian who reconstructs it. An appeal to it, therefore, cannot render an unbiased judgment. The literary critic would point to the language of the text itself and argue for the interpretation that most favorably abides by the textual and ideational constraints it imposes. Cultural studies argues, however, that those textual and ideational constraints are themselves filled with meaning potential that can be accessed in a multitude of appropriate ways. So who is right and who is wrong? The cultural studies proponent would argue that the case is always open, that readings are appropriate for particular cultures and come to life authoritatively in the midst of those cultures. We never really learn, in that case, which reading is the one objective and correct one. We learn instead how to comprehend the meaning of the text in vastly different and perhaps larger ways because we see and hear how others in their contextual situations access its meaning potential. As Segovia points out, that doesn't mean the text can be made to mean anything. In intercommunal conversation, the tension that arises between interpreters sharpens focus on the text and brings challenge to damaging, unsavory, and untenable readings. But such concluding challenges are not reached through an appeal to an arbitrary, standard, correct, and objective truth; they are reached in the crucible of communal conflict and conversation.

This is how culture reveals. Specifically. And this is why I now turn to an examination of African American church culture in my quest to construct a reading from the Apocalypse that might be intellectually meaningful and politically transformative for African American Christians and all others who are in community with them.

Chapter 2

Can I Get a Witness? An Apocalyptic Call for Active Resistance

The road toward the revitalization of theology is not via the escape of our culture, but the embodying of it self-consciously as we read the Bible, in order to see ourselves more clearly.[1]

*C*an I get a Witness?" "Can *I* get a Witness?" "Can I get a *Witness*?" I can't imagine that there is a single black churchgoer who is unfamiliar with this sermonic plea. Sometimes a plaintive groan, other times a defiant command, it is always a mark of high drama in the theater of African American worship. Whether the preacher is begging his audience to pay closer attention or demanding that they get up from their pews and transform their ritual attentiveness into discipleship endeavor, he uses this refrain the way a successful songwriter uses a "hook" phrase to catch her listeners' interest and get them quickly singing along. Peppered throughout the most climactic points of the sermon, it follows key words or phrases like a burst of fireworks, illuminating key homiletic themes. The preacher wants you not only to hear what he is saying but to understand and then to act upon it. "Didn't my Lord deliver Daniel? My Lord will deliver you, too! *Can* I Get a Witness?" "The same God who locked Satan *out* of heaven is going to lock him *up* in hell? Can *I* Get a Witness?" "God conquered Satan for *you*? Who are *you* going to conquer for God? Can I Get a *Witness*?"

37

In the book of Revelation, John is essentially asking the same question. A bit of a drama king himself, John knows how to catch and hold an audience. His visions, symbols, and hymns snare his readers with their larger-than-life imagery, while the constant message they embrace beats like an unforgettable worship refrain. *Jesus* is Lord! Jesus *is* Lord! Jesus is *Lord!* John's call to witness to that lordship is the religious, ethical, and very political expectation that naturally follows. This is what I see when I see John's Revelation through the lens of the Black Church. Revelation craves witness as engaged, resistant, transformative activism that is willing to sacrifice everything in an effort to make the world over into a reality that responds to and operates from Jesus' role as ruler and savior of all. In other words, "Jesus is Lord! *Can I get a Witness?*"

To be sure, this is not the way everyone sees it. Adela Yarbro Collins, for example, while agreeing that apocalyptic literature often both reflects and fosters a spirit of resistance, is not convinced that in Revelation John counsels his readers to act upon it. The Zealot, she says, provides an example of the visionary activist. Like John, the Zealots refused to acknowledge that Rome or Rome's Caesar had any claim to lordship over against their God. And, like John, they were willing to sacrifice everything to promote God's cause. As Elisabeth Schüssler Fiorenza observes, "the Jewish historian Josephus reports that like the souls crying out for justice [Rev. 6:9–11], the Zealots endured torture and execution rather than acknowledge the Roman emperor as sovereign."[2] The Zealots did more than endure, however; they acted. Convinced that they were working with God, they trusted that their resistant, revolutionary behavior was the human part of God's divine program to reinstitute God's rule. According to Collins, "this [Zealot] model might be called 'synergistic' in that both the Lord and the elect are thought to contribute to the victory."[3]

But, Collins would counter, John and his readers are no Zealots. At least not the "party" kind described by Josephus. Instead, John's charter membership was in what might be called the passive resistance party, of which there were two branches. The first branch followed the mandate set forth by the book of Daniel: "Wait and

See." Waiting and acting weren't necessarily mutually exclusive; it was just that only a certain kind of action was endorsed. One might "actively" endure the evils perpetrated against one by an oppressive power, but beyond that one stood fast. One waited to see when God would act and what God would do. The second branch, modeled on the narrative design of the *Assumption of Moses*, was like the first, except for a single, but nonetheless critical, distinction: "The behavior of the elect vis-à-vis the persecutor is the same, but a synergistic understanding of righteous suffering is introduced."[4] In this case, a believer didn't merely endure her suffering; she rejoiced privately in the knowledge that her suffering was in some way actually promoting God's own revolutionary cause. Though she herself did not change her world, her suffering spurred God on to do so. This is the way Collins would read John's call for resistance to Rome in Revelation. "The commitment to passive resistance is here combined with the idea of synergism inherent in the Israelite concept and practice of holy war. The synergism of the *Assumption of Moses* 9 is based on the confidence that the voluntary death of a righteous person will be avenged."[5] Since divine vengeance brings in the kingdom, those whose deaths sparked that vengeance will have played a passive role in the ushering in of God's revolutionary rule.

In making her case, Collins is as dualistic as the apocalyptic literature she studies: one is either a rabid revolutionary or an inert martyr; there is no middle ground. My perspective, filtered as it is through the Black Church tradition, offers an alternative view of the meaning potential bound up in John's apocalyptic imagery. The sensibility of apocalyptic synergism seems right; John does expect that human believers play a role in the execution of God's eschatological plan. I would argue, however, that while that role is not actively violent, neither is it passively compliant. There is a third way to read Revelation: as a call for active, nonviolent resistance. John summons this kind of behavior through his language of testimony. When he asks for a witness, he isn't interested in someone who just sits there and takes it; he is on the hunt for someone who will stand up and deliver.

Context Is Key: A Sociolinguistic Approach

A sociolinguistic approach to cultural studies gives methodological guidance to my reading of Revelation and helps shape my conclusion that John is calling for a witness of active, nonviolent resistance to Rome's claim of lordship over human history. Sociolinguistics urges that texts be viewed through the contexts in which they are shaped and read.[6] It is to those contexts, then, that I make my first interpretive turn. For my purposes here, there are three: the ancient cultural context in which the Apocalypse was first written and read; the contemporary cultural context in which I am now reading it; and, the larger literary context of the full narrative that gives shape to the particular texts that will draw our interest.

The Ancient Cultural Context:
The Emperor Cult and Asia Minor

Though some dissent remains, scholarship has come to the tentative conclusion that John's visionary prophecy was written at some point near the end of the last decade of the first century, during the reign of the emperor Domitian. Critical for our purposes is the manner in which the emperor and Rome were perceived religiously during this time in Asia Minor, where John's seven churches were located. In Rome's ideological infrastructure, religion and politics were quite intentionally mixed. Worship often mutated into politics; politics was often exercised through religion. Worship of Roman deities not only demonstrated a cultic devotion and communal piety, but also signaled loyalty to the Roman state that was mythologically connected to and founded upon them. It is not surprising, then, that the mother goddess would savor the name *Roma*, or that the messianic hopes for the empire should be bound up in the person of the emperor. Especially in Asia Minor, particularly during the last decade of the first century, emperor worship flourished. Schüssler Fiorenza is clear:

> Under the Flavians, especially Domitian, the imperial cult was strongly represented in the Roman provinces. Domitian

demanded that the populace acclaim him as "Lord and God" and participate in his worship. The majority of the cities to which the prophetic messages of Revelation are addressed were dedicated to the promotion of the emperor cult.[7]

On the issue of lordship, divine or otherwise, Christians had already staked out a rather intolerant, opposite claim: none other than Christ. Such a stance, in such a place, was bound to invite trouble. In such a place, if John is indeed demanding that his people witness publicly for the singular lordship of Jesus Christ, he would have to know that he is asking a lot. He would be asking them to resist. To resist Rome.

The Contemporary Cultural Context: The Black Church

I interpret that historical resistance through the lens of my very contemporary reading lens, the Black Church religious tradition. Before discussing that tradition and identifying the trait that most critically affects my reading of John's work, I want to clarify exactly what I mean by the term "Black Church." Following up from the work of C. Eric Lincoln, Lawrence H. Mamiya, and others,[8] Anthony Pinn offers a succinct definition. "The major denominations and smaller black denominations together constitute the Black Church. This does not mean that these various denominations are homogeneous. Nonetheless, this term—the Black Church—speaks to the vibrancy of a shared tradition of Christian commitment that has helped shape the collective black community."[9] Even though not all African American Christians are affiliated with the associations he goes on to mention (for example, he notes that there are over two million black Catholics), he formally identifies the Black Church with seven denominations: the African Methodist Episcopal Church; the African Methodist Episcopal Zion Church; the Christian Methodist Episcopal Church; the National Baptist Convention, U.S.A.; the National Baptist Convention of America; the Progressive National Baptist Convention; and the Church of God in Christ.[10] This 'magnificent seven' provides spiritual cover for approximately 80 percent of African American Christians.

Given the historical context out of which this Black Church emerged, it is not surprising that its spirituality has lived itself out in decidedly social and political ways. Lincoln and Mamiya state the historical case: "Two hundred and fifty years of slavery were followed by one hundred years of official and unofficial segregation in the South and in the North. Even today the gulf still persists, bolstered in large measure by racial segregation in the place of residence, education, religion, and social life."[11] Peter Paris goes further. This oppressive circumstance, he argues, wasn't merely the context out of which the Black Church arose; it was the reason for its genesis: as he puts it, "racism and racial self-respect have been the two warring principles that caused the emergence of the black churches."[12]

At every critical stage in its existence, the Black Church has preoccupied itself with the task of finding a way to respond appropriately to the racially charged context that conceived it and gave it birth. Spiritually, it has preached a message of equality before God. Socially and politically, it has demanded that this spiritual reality acquire concrete communal expression. And it has striven to enact it. As Pinn puts it, "during its more than 250 years of existence, the Black Church, when at its best, has developed forms of praxis geared toward addressing the terror and dread of objectification through the nurturing of sociopolitically and economically vital and vibrant Americans, who exercise all the rights and responsibilities endemic to full citizenship."[13] Of all the traits that might be used to describe the Black Church, then, the one that might be considered its most enduring, constant, and characteristic would be its drive toward the uplift and thus liberation of its people.

Clearly, "liberation" was a key principle in the life of the slave church. In a world where owners punished slaves for participating in unauthorized and unsupervised worship services in the late night woods or slave quarter root cellars, the very act of worship was an expression of political defiance. Under threat of severe repercussions, slaves persisted in their desires to use their clandestine worship services as opportunities to beg for God's liberating intervention in their lives. Slave preachers and singers dramatized this liberation emphasis in their sermons and lyrics.[14] Slave insurrectionists drew the connections even more sharply. Like John, they believed God would use any means at God's disposal, including revolutionary violence, to reach God's emancipatory goal for all God's people. According to Lincoln and Mamiya, "American historians of slavery often tend to overlook the fact that the three largest slave revolts in American history were led by slave preachers, who used their status as religious leaders to mobilize thousands of African slaves."[15]

During the period following slavery, from the latter part of the nineteenth century on into the early twentieth century, there was retrenchment in the liberative thinking and activism of the Black Church. As Pinn observes, however, even during this more conservatively pietistic phase, "the otherworldly orientation did not lose sight of dehumanization as evil."[16] While some churches continued efforts of social and political activism, others, focused on the rewards of the heavenly world, directed their energies toward the spiritual condition of African Americans. And yet, even here, there was a liberative emphasis. Pinn concludes: "The difference, then, involves liberation through spiritual means over against liberation through forms of societal engagement."[17] In very many cases, concrete social results evolved from spiritual preoccupation. "Black churches developed a variety of social services including libraries, job training, basic education programs, and health care programs. And these activities on the part of black churches speak to an appreciation for a social form of Christianity that is sensitive to the changing cultural and social realities encountered by black Americans."[18]

The civil rights movement provided an illustrative example of the Black Church's commitment to social and political liberation. According to Pinn, "in addition to providing bodies willing to participate in direct action, disseminate information, and finance protest activities, the Black Church also provided the ideological and theological underpinning for the movement."[19] The black theology movement followed from and built upon this ideological emphasis. Indeed, Pinn can argue that "It is with this theological shift [to black theology] that liberation is most forcefully presented as a metaphor for the Black Church's work."[20] Following in the historical footsteps of the slave insurrectionists and apparently in the theological footsteps of the apocalyptist John, black theology advocates were not convinced that God couldn't and wouldn't use violence as a means to institute God's ultimate goal of liberating all humans from oppression. Pinn therefore notes that "while some objected to its failure to denounce violence as a legitimate means of protest, black clergy and professional scholars who advocated black theology—such figures as J. Deotis Roberts, James Cone, and Gayraud Wilmore—maintained God's participation in the struggle against injustice, arguing that reconciliation without liberation (or justice) was impossible."[21]

The 1990s saw a dramatic shift in the economic circumstance of the Black Church. Individual churches became much more affluent, and black ministers solidly established themselves in the ranks of the comfortable middle class. Pinn and other scholars of the Black Church are concerned that, as a result, the Black Church has become focused more on matters of individual piety than issues of social and political justice. They are also concerned about the self-serving way in which the church has applied its freedom focus. "The ethic generating this outlook and activity was played out on the collective level, although in imperfect and often inconsistent ways, as the sexism, homophobia, and heterosexism of most black churches demonstrates."[22] And yet they remain convinced, it seems, that the emphasis on liberation is so strongly ingrained in the church's being that it will remain the driving force that may transform its own corporate existence, even as it seeks to transfigure the society that surrounds it. And so Paris argues that "[the Black Church's] basic source of authority has been that to which they have been unreservedly committed, namely, a biblical anthropology which they believe strongly affirms the equality of all persons under God regardless of race or any other natural quality. This doctrine has been the essence of the black Christian tradition and the most fundamental requirement of its churches."[23] Andrew Billingsley agrees: "But in the black church, despite the millions of sermons preached, the prayers prayed, the solemn spiritual songs lifted up to heaven, freedom is as burning an issue today as it was when God first revealed Himself and His true relationship to His black children in America."[24]

Lincoln and Mamiya not only concur, they give an operational definition to what they and I believe most scholars of the Black Church mean when they talk about liberation: "From the very beginning of the black experience in America, one critical denotation of freedom has remained constant: freedom has always meant the absence of any restraint which might compromise one's responsibility to God."[25] Pinn not only approves of this contention; he extends it. For him, it is not only the case that the Black Church has harbored a consistent emphasis on liberation; by the actions of its adherents, it has also demonstrated the firm belief that black people could participate with God in bringing that liberation about. "Although applied imperfectly, this ethic of liberation was meant to forge what might be referred to as responsible selves, able to exercise agency in ways that transform existing sociopolitical structures."[26] This "agency" operates from the same principle of synergy that, according to Collins, the first-century apocalyptic writers believed was the connection between their efforts and God's.

It is just here, of course, that we can see how the liberative emphasis of the Black Church corresponds quite provocatively with the witness of resistance that John calls for in his Roman context of Asia Minor at the end of the first century. If Billingsley is right, the Black Church and the Apocalypse target the same objective. "The freedom the black church has been after . . . is the freedom to belong to God, to worship God exclusively, and it is the freedom to participate in the divine agenda without selective hindrance from other human beings."[27] If my suspicions and Collins's claims about synergy are correct, John trusted that his believers could and should work with God to bring about that objective. The question is, were they working for this liberation through their suffering, or were they witnessing so actively for this liberation that suffering was bound to occur? Collins believes the former. The more I read Revelation through the lens of the Black Church, the more I am convinced of the latter.

The Literary Context: Witness Ethics

I am convinced because of the way John uses his witness language. He deliberately encodes it with the symbolism of religious and political disobedience. It makes perfect sense that someone reading his visionary prophecy through the double lens of John's late-first-century, Asia Minor context and the historical context of the Black Church tradition would decode that imagery as a call for active, nonviolent, engaged resistance.

Why? This master of the metaphor surely must have considered the range of meaning that would have been available to his readers when they came into contact with his linguistic symbols. He would have wanted to know what possible conclusions they might draw from his use of particular words. To know that, he'd need to be aware, as aware we need to be, of the range of meaning that was available for a particular word in the particular time he was using it. What did a person at the end of the first century hear when someone like John used the words *testimony, testify,* or *witness?*

The answer to this question is critical for our contemporary interpretive efforts, because *martys,* the Greek term for "witness," has come to mean something quite different from what it meant for John and his hearers and readers. The confusion is contextual. When we transliterate the Greek letters of *martys* into their corresponding Roman letters we see and hear the word *martyr.* We have seen and heard it for more than nineteen centuries. The problem is that the transliteration of the word in the twenty-first century means something different from what the word itself meant at the end of the first century. H. Strathmann testifies that for John and his hearers, "the proper sphere of *martus* is the legal, where it denotes one who can and does speak from personal experience about actions in which he took part and which happened to him, or about persons and relations known to him."[28] Allison Trites offers clear corroboration: "The idea of witness in the Apocalypse is very much a live metaphor and is to be understood in terms of Christians actually bearing witness before Roman courts of law."[29] It is a word of active engagement, not sacrificial passivity. Indeed, the image of prophecy probably conjures the better meaning parallel. The witness of Christians might provoke such a hostile response that it leads to their deaths, but always—at least in the first-century mindset it seems—the transformative focus was on the provocative testimony that had to be given, not a passive life that had to be extinguished. And so Fred Mazzaferri can argue that "the paramount stress of *martyrs* is therefore prophetic, not martyrological."[30] In other words, when someone in John's turn-of-the-first-century environment said *witness*, she meant witness, not martyr.

John spells out the *kind* of witness he encourages through his key characterizations. The foundational role is played by the Lamb. On first glance, the Lamb imagery seems to fit the latter-day martyr image. After all, its key signification is the mark of its slaughter, which John introduces in chapter 5. Interestingly enough, though, well before John characterizes Jesus as the Lamb, he identifies him at 1:5, by name, as *the* faithful *witness*. At 3:14, still before any mention of the Lamb, comes linguistic reinforcement; as witness, Jesus is both faithful and true.[31] There is no need for interpretation; John has made his point clearly. Whatever else he might appear to be to his followers, Jesus Christ is first and foremost God's prime witness. Every other characterization must be interpreted in that light, and not the other way around. The question we are narratively driven to ask, then, is this: how are we to understand the Lamb's slaughter in the light of his role as God's faithful witness? That is to say, what is it about his witness that connects with and perhaps even causes his killing? The implication from the end-of-the-first-century, Asia Minor context is suggestive; Jesus, *the* prophetic witness figure, apparently testified to a truth. He faithfully adhered to that testimony even under the direst of circumstances, at the cost of his own life. Clarification comes from the cross. As Trites notes: "From the context of the Apocalypse as a whole, it seems probable that *the witness of Jesus* (*hē marturia Iēsou*) in these passages refers primarily to Christ's passion, where he witnessed 'the good confession' before Pontius Pilate (cf. I Tim. vi 13)."[32] What could that confession be in the narrative of John's Revelation other than the proclamation of cosmic and human lordship that follows directly upon the rhetorical heels of Jesus' introduction as *the* faithful witness (1:4–8)? We will find that this declaration was as dangerous a testimony for a Christian believer to make in John's time as it had been so obviously disastrous for Jesus to have made in his own.

John's literary self-portrait as an eager witness to Jesus' own testimonial of lordship is a forbidding case in point. He has been actively testifying to that lordship and, as the literary evidence of his Apocalypse confirms (see chapters 2–3), recruiting others to do the same. There are two noteworthy points about John's self-presentation. First, he characterizes himself not only as their brother, but as their partner in tribulation. The partner language is an invitation to imitation; John wants them to be as related by their behavior as they are bonded by their faith. Significantly, the one behavior that he has highlighted thus far is the behavior of witness. And when he finally singles out one of their number, Antipas, one of his "brothers" in the faith and partners in crime, it is his faithful witness, which linguistically mimics that of Jesus, that he lauds. John wants them to follow his and Antipas's lead. Even knowing the dangers, he wants them to stick their necks out and witness to the lordship of Christ. This does not sound all that passive to me.

Second, as expected, John has paid a heavy price. When John in 1:9 uses the phrase "because of" (*dia* plus a following object in the accusative case) he does so to refer to the result of an action. John has been banished to Patmos as a direct result of his preaching the Word of God and the testimony of Jesus.[33] In staking his claim about the reasons for his incarceration, John has also correlated and defined his key terms. The "and" (*kai*) that stands between the two terms is epexegetical. That is to say, the "and" means the two words point to the same reality, not to two different ones. When John says, "the word of God and the witness of Jesus Christ," he means, "the word of God, *which is* the witness of Jesus Christ." Further, the two genitive constructions, word *of* God and witness *of* Jesus, are subjective genitives. John is talking about the word shared by God and the witness borne by Jesus. The end equation, then, is rather plain: God's word and Jesus' witness are the same thing.[34]

The critical question is this: what *is* God's word, which is Jesus' testimony? Put simply, it is that Christ is Lord. John intentionally places grammatical infelicities in his narrative so that the point he desires to make with them will stand out. After a careful reader's attention has been snared by the blunder, she will notice the more important point that the blunder marks. In this particular case, at that critical point of 1:5, where John introduces Jesus as the faithful witness, he goes on to characterize him as "the firstborn of the dead and the ruler of the kings of the earth." Since *witness, firstborn,* and *ruler* are all modifying the noun *Jesus Christ,* which is in the genitive, they should all be in the genitive, too. John, however, has, right at the start of his work, committed a major writing faux pas; he has put the adjectives in the nominative case instead. He might as well be a contemporary bishop or moderator who has begun the first paragraph of a major church paper with sentences whose plural subjects are followed up by singular verbs. Who takes a writer seriously when he starts out with sentences like "We is the church of God"? John apparently believes that, before dismissing him, his suddenly attentive readers, who are also convinced of his literary skill, will wonder whether the slip is really a slip. Their reward: they will recognize that he is following the logic of Psalm 89:37 (LXX 88:38), where the same modifiers are also all in the nominative and all point in the direction of David's throne. In other words, after reading 1:5 in light of Psalm 89:37, John's hearers and readers will realize that Jesus' description as faithful witness also defines him as the firstborn among the kings of the earth.[35] Indeed, that *is* his witness; that *is* God's word. As God is the ruler of all, *pantocrator,* Jesus is the ruler of the entire human realm. That is the revelation of Jesus Christ.[36] That is the testimony to which they are to give active witness.

Three Test Cases

How do we know this witness is *active*? By tracking John's use of the term and the way he relates it to the work of his hearers and readers. In this short book, I am not interested in all of John's witness language. I focus instead on those texts where he packages "witness" with word of God and then causally connects them both to some form of reactionary persecution. In 1:9, it was John's exile. In 6:9–11; 12:10–12; and 20:4–6, it will be his followers' deaths. The fact that punishment occurs as a result of witnessing implies that the witnessing is an active, public enterprise. Whether done in response to hostile inquiry by community leaders or voluntarily as a spontaneous act of faith declaration, witnessing appears very much to be a live action endeavor.

We need not deal any longer with 1:9, since the very existence of John's written Apocalypse sufficiently testifies to the fact that he was actively promoting the lordship of Jesus Christ and enlisting others to do so as well, despite the acknowledged cost. Even if one were to come to the conclusion that all John's hearers and readers were passive, and that he counseled them to be so, one could not make the same claim about John himself. He was a prophet who preached and disseminated the dangerous message he believed. And if he was indeed presenting himself as a kind of model witness, it would seem natural to suggest that he expected them to stand up and deliver the prophetic word about Jesus' lordship in the same way that he himself was delivering it.

But was he? That is the question now. Did he get his hearers and listeners to follow his lead? Were they as actively defiant as John was himself?

6:9–11 Tortured Witness

They were. John declares in the very next combined use of our key terminology that souls who had been slaughtered on earth because of the word of God, which is the testimony of Jesus, were crammed into the crawl space beneath the heavenly altar, crying out for God's justice. Location, location, location! For some scholars, their presence under the altar is an indication that John has in mind sacrificial, martyr imagery.[37] These scholars refer to the Leviticus 4:7 text, where the blood of a sacrificial bull is poured out at the base of the altar. Since the life or soul was in the blood, they argue, John was symbolically representing the souls as the blood of the altar poured out. In this case, these slaughtered souls sacrificed themselves so that by their bloody deaths they would provoke God's final intervention into human history. Therein, then, lies the synergy. It is their deaths that matter, not necessarily what they did that caused those deaths.

I am not so sure. I would argue instead for the primacy of another part of the altar's meaning potential: justice and judgment. Just as the throne is a symbol of God's rule, the altar, at least in Revelation, characterizes God's judgment. After all, John does not picture a sacrificial slaying on the altar; the slaying, presumably with all the accompanying bleeding, takes place on earth. John images the altar to picture what will now happen *as a result* of the slaying. In other words, the altar represents not the killing but the divine response to it. In 8:3 we find helpful corroboration. There, on the incense altar, the prayers of the saints are offered without any indication of blood or suffering at all; but the connection to the coming judgment is clear. At 16:7, the altar is so focused on this objective that it miraculously comes alive and voices the opinion that all God's judgments are true and just. Indeed, all of John's representations of the heavenly temple fit this symbolic mold (8:3, 5; 9:13; 14:18; 16:7); they are connected to divine recompense, not saintly suffering. Even the slaughtered souls are convinced of this connection. Apparently certain that God will act, their interrogative concerns the timing of the event. They are asking when, not if. The symbolism of the altar assures them that transformative, liberating justice is coming. This is why John locates them there; he wants his readers to be more focused on God's justice than on their own sacrifice.

If that is so, one might rightfully counter, why did John characterize the souls as "slaughtered"? Does not that description, connected as it is with blood and altar imagery, imply sacrifice? To be sure, that is a part of the meaning potential; I am not arguing that it is not. I am pressing the case that there is more. After all, Jesus too, as the Lamb, was characterized as slaughtered. As narrated by John, though, his slaughtering was to be understood in terms of his witnessing. By marking the souls with the same trait that so highlighted Jesus' symbolic person, John is demonstrating how much they have become like him. Like him, they have been killed because of their fidelity to the word of Jesus' lordship that Jesus himself so heroically bore. The primacy of place, historically and figuratively, then, belongs to that heroism; without it there would be no motivation for slaughtering.

Collins and others have pointed out that John was not writing during a period of wanton persecution, during which Christ believers were persecuted on a wide and irrational scale, as they had been during Nero's time. In the time when John wrote, persecutions were targeted affairs; they were deployed as a result of a particular kind of obstinacy. They were used because fools like John kept witnessing to a dangerous truth they believed was worth suffering for and perhaps even dying for. Preaching the lordship of Christ might just ultimately make it so. John obviously believed it; the Romans apparently feared it. Why else punish such witness so? The focus was on the witnessing; the slaughtering was just one of the many possible responses. It just happened to be the response that was particular to the souls crammed under the crawl space of the heavenly altar.

White slave owners in the American South were caught in the same predicament as the Romans. They didn't believe in the liberating, transformative power of slave religion. Why, then, did they outlaw its free expression and punish it so?[38] Why would enforcers of segregation and Jim Crow so viciously punish witnesses to the equality of all before God decades later? When one looked at the sacrifices of the slaves and their later freed and freeborn brothers and sisters, would one's transformative focus be on their dying or on their "witnessing" to their faith? Martin Luther King Jr. is not one of the most significant figures in the history of the twentieth century because he was assassinated. He is significant because he witnessed to a message of transformative equality that so threatened America's segregated way of life that an agent of that way sought to kill the message by slaughtering him. The principal focus, though, has always been on what King did, not that King died. Slaves who were brutalized and killed, free blacks who were strung up and lynched were also no doubt slaughtered souls occupying real estate beneath the heavenly altar. To be sure, African Americans spoke and do still speak of the horrors endured by their ancestors and even now by their brothers and sisters. And yet it is not the slaughter that they emphasize. Do they moralize slaughter, spiritualize it, make it somehow redemptive or transformative? Is that the part of the meaning potential that becomes most meaningful for them? Pinn thinks not:

> The sense of terror or dread prompted by these rituals gave rise to the historical manifestation of religiosity. By this I do not mean rhetorical appeals to the sacred commonly found on the lips of those in pain and despair. Rather, promoting a sense of religious human construction, I argue that this dread sparks the development of practices, doctrines, and institutional structures earmarked for historical liberation from terror.[39]

In other words, it may well be that readers operating from such a Black Church tradition, as Pinn here lays out, might see in this horrific scenario of slaughtered souls a symbolic call to respond to terror in ways that might help (synergy) bring about God's justice more quickly. Could it be that this portrait of butchered witnesses was less a ritual celebration of sacrifice than it was a visceral call for prophetic engagement? Pinn goes on: "This is not to suggest, however, that this terror or dread is a 'positive' or useful thing simply because it results in manifestations of religion. . . . Instead, this terror or dread are historical realities that must be fought."[40]

Like black folk huddled before pictures and stories of mutilated runaways or lynched relatives, the horror was not remembered so as to be found redemptive; it was remembered so as to provoke action, perhaps the kind of action that might, before it brought transformation, well result in even more of the slaughter. Perhaps that is why John pictures the souls crying out beneath the altar: not to instill a sense of religious wonder, but to shore up and ignite a furious and active resolve. In the end, the same irony overwhelmed the purveyors of racial hatred in America that overwhelmed the Romans; slaughter brought more witness, not less. Perhaps John knew all along that it would. What better reason to showcase that slaughter so?

Even the crying out was, just as it had been for the Hebrew psalmist and prophets, a worship way of witnessing to the presence and power of God.[41] Even as they lamented, they fought back. They called to God, their *despotēs*. David Aune clarifies that *despotēs* is a regular Greek translation of the two Latin terms for emperor, a point that would certainly not have gone unnoticed.[42] In crying out to God as their *despotēs*, they were rhetorically slapping Caesar in the face. Even in their desperation, then, they were actively engaged.

So were African American Christians in the Black Church tradition. Their worship, even in the direst of circumstances, was a witness to the contrary and transformative lordship of Christ. Like Rome, the slave system promoted its own lordship and sought to squelch any expression of slave faith to the contrary. JoAnne Marie Terrell writes poignantly about "the paternalistic ethos in which slavocracy was shrouded, and the ways it sacralized the slaveholders," and she relays the testimony of a former slave: "Alex Woods attests to the thinly veiled idolatry of the slaveholders in the exercise of their authority: 'Dey wouldn't allow 'em to call on de Lord when dey were whippin' 'em, but dey let 'em say, 'Oh, pray! Oh, pray, Marster!'"[43]

Given such a context, any expression of unauthorized worship by slaves was an expression of resistance. Speaking of slave devotions, Pinn writes: "By violating regulations against unsupervised gatherings, those participating in hush-arbor meetings addressed the terror of slave status through an exercise of will. . . . In other words, unmonitored gatherings would result in blacks using religious doctrine to challenge the social order."[44] Terrell would appear to agree. The shouting out of brutalized slaves in worship, analogous in many ways to the crying out of these slaughtered souls in Revelation, in and of itself was a register not of futility but defiance. "Shouting among the slaves and their descendants was/is literally and figuratively a *seizure* of human agency and artistic freedom, a melodramatic response to the absurdity of their life conditions."[45] As Terrell implies, this defiant emphasis continued into the worship of the Black Church: "The Black Church as a manifestation of religion responds to terror by seeking to

establish blacks as agents of will; Christian gatherings orches-
trated by churches served as a ritual of 'exorcism' in that they fos-
tered a break with status as will-less objects and encouraged new
forms of relationship and interaction premised upon black inten-
tionality."[46] Looking through the lens of this African American
worship tradition, one comes to view the meaning potential of
6:9–11 in a quite different, activist light. Even the "how long,
Lord," which might otherwise be interpreted as the passive cry of
the utterly helpless, becomes a testimony to the belief that "we
know it won't be long, *true* Lord and Master, before you engage
our world, and with our help make it right."[47]

Even the manner in which John gives these souls symbolic
identity highlights them as defiant witnesses actively engaged in
their own uplift through their preaching of the lordship of Christ.
Before the heavenly voice answers their worship request, John
tells us that they were given white robes. As J. P. Heil points out,
they are connected by their dress to other key characterizations in
the text.[48] The multitude standing before the Lamb and the heavenly throne in 7:9 are similarly dressed. So, interestingly enough,
are the figures of 7:13 and 14. These figures, presumably the same
folk as our slaughtered souls of 6:9–11, achieved their high laun-
dry marks only after washing their robes in the blood of the Lamb.
According to 12:10–12, this high powered plasma detergent is the
cleansing force that enables God and God's people to wipe out
the stain of Rome's oppressive, satanic power. The white robe is
the static symbolization of this ongoing wash cycle.

In other words, the white robe, metaphorically speaking, is not
a noun; it is an action verb. The robe signifies the washing in the
blood that brings about the transformative justice God's people
have been seeking. They haven't just been "given" white robes;
they have earned them by washing, that is, acting in the way of the
Lord. That way, we have already learned, is a witnessing to his
own lordship that causes his own death, just as it caused John's
exile to Patmos. Surely this active witness is what John has in mind
at 3:4–5, when he declares that the remnant at Sardis have earned
their white dress because of their ongoing and victorious witness. Who, finally, are the ones whom John considers blessed and

worthy of the liberating salvation that God will bring? Who else but those who act, who "wash" their robes. The only mechanism by which John makes this "washing" possible is that of witnessing to the very truth that Rome has deployed all its power to contest. Their very dress, then, symbolizes active, perhaps even bloody, engagement, not passive acceptance.

This is exactly the kind of identity issue that resonates in the Black Church tradition, where the wearing of distinctive clothing and what Pinn calls the presentation of the body was itself often a symbol of transformation and triumph. Pinn argues that "the public presentation of black bodies reflected comportment and thereby was understood as an extension of moral and ethical conduct."[49] Dress was as symbolic of action as it was of identity. How did this develop? The slave owner had a way of dressing slaves only in the essentials necessary to any given task. Slaves were well dressed only during those times when it suited the owner, for example, when they were placed on an auction block and paraded about like a cleaned-up plantation tool. By controlling appearance the owner demonstrated his symbolic control over the slave.

In John's narrative, the Romans have an equally powerful code of dress, a one-size-fits-all kind of symbolic garment: the accoutrements of slaughter. The Romans controlled when believers would wear it and how often. They therefore demonstrated that, despite what a believer believed, Rome controlled him or her too.

The African American slave used contraband opportunities to dress up for special occasions and for services of worship, whether in clothes bought by the owner or not, as a gesture of independence and defiance. This defiance remained a strong part of the Black Church tradition. "Hence, in the Black Church, clothing was not a sign of one's value for others as their objects; rather, it was a sign of one's value for oneself, one's community, and one's God."[50] The dress became a form of witness. "By decorating the body in this manner, blacks forced their visibility and reshaped social space, the social environment."[51] Dressing up became an active form of protest and transformative challenge.

Reading the desire of John's believers to wash their fine white robes in the blood of the Lamb through this African American lens elicits a powerfully new way of accessing the meaning potential of John's apocalyptic dress code. Pinn argues for what he calls "a dissonance between the social body and the black bodies, a discord that sparks and fuels religion as historical liberation because the former operates through a process of bad faith and corrupt intentions."[52] One could argue for the same dissonance between the social body (expectation of emperor worship) and the witness body or "soul" (which symbolizes resistance to that expectation) in Revelation. The Roman system promotes a celebration of the physical body and physical life lived in accommodation to Roman religious and political interest. Revelation symbolizes a rejection of that hold on the physical body. It is not the body but the redressed and eternal *psychē* that is key. This spiritual body is, of course, in extreme dissonance with the Roman social one. By definition, it is therefore resistant, and actively so.

A believer must make an active choice, given the social context of Asia Minor at the end of the first century, to be one type of body or the other. John dramatizes his preference with the description of slaughtered souls clothed in white robes. He has essentially reconfigured the dress of slaughter into the clothing of defiance and change. He takes even the worst, this slaughter, and linguistically connects it as closely to Christ's resurrection as to his death. The slaughtered Lamb, every reader will remember, was still standing. So too is the believer who takes the wardrobe of Christ's slaughter upon him or herself. Though huddled beneath the heavenly altar, the believers are well dressed and, figuratively speaking at least, still standing. All of a sudden, what some might view as a martyr's attire has become the fine, white linen of active, subversive, transformative witness. These dead souls, all dressed up, are a soul force.

On the surface, the answer the heavenly voice speaks to this soul force appears to cause a problem for the thesis I am suggesting. After all, the respondent directs that the pleading souls should wait just a short time until the appropriate number of their brothers (and sisters) have, like them, been killed.[53] Actually, the Greek says no such thing. Although the NRSV and many other translations report that a sufficient *number* of witnesses first had to be slaughtered before God would move, John himself actually says nothing about any number. He simply writes that first the brothers and sisters must be fulfilled. Admittedly, this odd response is rather ambiguous. It is not surprising that translators and interpreters sought clarification from the context. Aune makes the historical observation that apocalyptic texts like 1 Enoch 47:4 and 4 Ezra 4:35–37 expect a certain quota of slaughtered righteous to be fulfilled before God will act.[54] In this case, believers can be in synergy with God by acting as sacrifices that provoke God's behavior.

Mitchell G. Reddish agrees that John probably has this apocalyptic concept in mind, but he is not so sure that John wants to use it to the same effect as his literary forebears. He writes: "Whether John took literally this idea of a fixed number of martyrs who must die before God intervenes is not clear. The freedom he exhibits elsewhere to adapt and modify ancient traditions and to cast ideas in symbolic form leads one to suspect that here also he is using a traditional apocalyptic idea in a nonliteral way."[55] I would agree. Especially since John, whose idea of a martyr is that of a witness, left out any talk of a "number" at all. John's concentration is focused on the term "fulfill" (*plēroō*).

Gerhard Delling instructs that *fulfill*, particularly when connected with the term *time* (*chronos*) has a temporal sense of completion. It other words, it means to finish, to execute a commanded action; "almost always [it is] God's commission which is to be fulfilled."[56] That broader use of the term fits quite nicely with the way John uses the term in 3:2, the only other time he deploys it. There, *fulfill* is used in the sense of works. The Lord is angry because the works of the believers have not been "accomplished" in the Lord's sight. All this would suggest that when John uses *fulfill* in 6:11, particularly in relationship to rest (from works?) and time, he is speaking about the works of the colleagues of the slaughtered souls. He highlights the work of defiant, provocative witness that must be accomplished, however that is to be done. Doing that work is the way believers operate in synergy with God to bring about the liberating transformation of history.

Corroboration comes from John's closing remark about the brothers and sisters who would be killed, just as the souls themselves had been. We already know that the souls were slaughtered because of their witness; John is clarifying here that their brothers and sisters will be slaughtered for the same reason. Nonetheless, they apparently are to keep witnessing until their work is complete. When will that be? Pinn offers a response that is as appropriate for John as it is for the African American Christian in the Black Church tradition: "There is no certainty, no way of knowing our efforts will have long-term benefits or sustained merit. But this is not the point. In this system of ethics, the goal of social activism [witnessing?], or struggle [slaughter?], is concerned with fostering space, broadly defined, in which we can undertake the continual process of rethinking ourselves."[57] In other words, we are not to see ourselves as passive victims, but, even as we wait and worship, as active witnesses to a transforming lordship that transfigures us and our world even as and *precisely because* we witness to it.

20:4 Triumphant Witness

That transfiguration comes full circle in John's narration at 20:4. Clearly 6:9 and 20:4 are linked. Aune diagrams the indisputable connection; except for the addition of the altar imagery and the place switching of *word* and *witness*,[58] 6:9 and 20:4 are for a large part structural parallels.[59] Both texts reference souls who have been killed because of their commitment to the word of God that is the witness borne by Jesus. In chapter 6, John says the souls were slaughtered; in 20:4, he specifies that the butchery took place as beheadings. Aune clarifies that John is talking about the same characters: "It is more natural to construe the text as referring to a single group of martyrs, who had been executed for both positive reasons (v. 4b: their obedience to the commands of God and their witness to Jesus) and negative concerns (v. 4c: their refusal to worship the beast or its image and to receive its brand on their foreheads and right hands)."[60] It would be even less cumbersome to explain that, since the souls represent the same group of believers, they are also being killed for the same obstinate witness. That is to say, their obedience to the word of God and refusal to worship the beast *are* the ways they witness to Jesus. Their commitment to

Jesus' own testimony of his lordship (the positive) requires that they likewise refuse any form of worshipping the reality or power of the beast (the negative). It is all witness for John.

Despite the parallelism, John does give his hearers and readers something new here. The souls' death-causing witness leads paradoxically to triumph rather than to defeat. At 6:9, the souls were crying out for justice; at 20:4, they get it. Like Jesus following his death on the cross, they are raised triumphantly beyond their slaughter to take their places with God on heavenly thrones so as, in a case of cosmic synergy this time, to work judgment with God.[61] The Romans' reactionary hostility belied their fear that witness to Jesus' lordship would transfigure their reality. Now the very thing they wanted to stop has come about, precisely *because of* their vicious attempts to stop it. Here, at the opening of 20:4, John declares that this cosmic transfiguration has indeed taken place. Before the verse ends, he proclaims that it has occurred on earth as well. These slaughtered souls recapture life and reign with Christ for a thousand years.[62]

12:10–12 Victorious Witness

Something is, of course, missing. How did these witnessing souls get from the here of historical slaughter and heavenly wailing to the there of cosmic kingship and earthly rule? I believe John tells us in his redrafting of the cosmic combat myth that is chapter 12. Once again there are structural clues that point a way forward. William Shea is convinced that chapters 12 and 20 are structurally parallel.[63] I am focused, of course, on the particular similarities between 20:4 and any material in chapter 12. Shea notes that 12:6 and 12:13–16 form exactly the same kind of highlighting inclusion around 12:7–12 as 20:3 and 20:7 form around 20:4–6.[64] In each case, material of signal importance is being showcased. This suggests some type of correspondence between the two key sections, 12:7–12 and 20:4–6. One verse in chapter 12 contains the same key characterizations and terminology that I have been exploring thus far. At 12:11, John includes all of our vital witness language: *souls*, *word*, and *witness*. He even ties them all together with the theme of causality. As Shea concludes: "It seems evident that the intent of the text is to refer to the same group through the use of the same terminology in all three cases."[65] The twist this time is that the witness of these death-defying, blood-soaked souls is causally linked not with death, but with victory.

In chapter 12 John is reconfiguring the ancient formula of a cosmic combat myth to place Jesus in the role of messianic heir.[66] Just as John usurps titles normally meant for Caesar and tauntingly delivers them to Jesus, so here he co-opts a myth used in Roman religious contexts to depict the emperor as a divine. According to John's telling, Jesus, not the emperor, is the real subject of this mythological presentation. Jesus, not the emperor, is the cosmic and historical Lord who defeats the force of evil and establishes order and justice. Even in his storytelling, John is a defiant witness!

There is more! It is not just that Jesus is the true Lord; those who witness to Jesus' lordship, by doing so, help make that lordship occur. Their historical testimony has cosmic significance; it will help bring Rome down as it assists God in raising Jesus up. So Reddish explains:

> The primeval chaos monster has reared its ugly head again, this time in Roman dress. By painting their problems on a cosmic canvas, John is giving added meaning and significance to their struggles. Theirs is no minor or inconsequential skirmish, but another battle in the ongoing conflict that has existed since primeval times. By their faithfulness to God, they are helping to defeat the powers of evil.[67]

They are helping to defeat Rome. According to 12:11, that assistance occurs not because of their deaths, but because of their active, resistant witness against Rome's lordship claims.

John retells the myth simply enough. In verses 1–4a, two key characters are introduced, the woman clothed with the sun who will give birth to the messianic child, and the dragon who would do anything to slaughter her offspring. Verses 4b–6 catalogue the child's birth and escape to the throne of God, after which the woman flees to the sanctuary of the wilderness. In the next major movement of the story, verses 7–12, the dragon is defeated after a raging battle in heaven. The story closes with verses 13–17, which describe the dragon's final pursuit of the woman and her other, subsequent offspring.[68] The key part of the story for us is the hymn of verses 10–12, which not only celebrates the dragon's defeat but offers commentary on it. I conclude from that commentary two key points.

First, chapter 12 is a part of a larger story flashback that provides a rationale for Rome's hostility toward John's believers and the testimony they are charged to bear.[69] Though it follows chapters 4–11, which focus on the introduction of the Lamb, the breaking of the seven seals, the blowing of the seven trumpets, and the work of the two witnesses, it thematically precedes them.[70] Indeed, the chapter's conclusion appears more to start a story than to end one. As Aune puts it, "Since Rev 12 ends before the story has been satisfactorily concluded, it must be regarded as the first 'move,' with other moves to follow."[71] I agree. And I want to push his observation to its logical conclusion.

In chapters 1–11, Satan is clearly wreaking havoc through Rome on earth. And yet, when chapter 12 opens, Satan is still in heaven; everything chronicled here in the chapter's opening verses, then, must have happened well before the chaos taking place in chapters 1–11. In fact, chapters 1–11 feel much more like the kind of activity that John describes taking place after chapter 12 comes to a close. It is only after the dragon launches a futile attempt from his heavenly perch to destroy the messianic child figure and subsequently finds himself in cosmic exile, that he turns in pursuit of the other children, the metaphorical church. But the story of that pursuit is the point at which John opens his apocalypse in chapter 1. In other words, chapter 12 *ends* at the place where the book of Revelation *begins*.

If I am right, chapter 12 sets up and explains everything that has narratively come before it. That is because the events in chapter 12 have happened before everything that narratively precedes it. It therefore provides the motivation for the anger Rome feels towards the Lamb and the witness to his lordship. It provides our window into the truth that Rome knows and fears: Jesus is the coming messianic figure whose cosmic lordship will soon be revealed on earth. Nowhere in John's work to this point has it been said why this testimony of these witnesses is so inflammatory. Latter-day Christians immediately presume a rationale from their faith context. But if we read John without resorting to that particular faith bias, we come away wondering why Rome should care enough that the proclamations of this troublesome small sect would warrant such imperial concern. In chapter 12, John explains why by mythologically flashing back to the beginning to give us some perspective. The next section, 13–15:4, will explain who that dragon is and connect it historically with Rome, but chapter 12 tells us why that dragon has so much vested in stopping these witnesses and the testimony they convey. It must stifle the coming cosmic truth that their witnessing is helping to bring about. Why? Because, according to 12:11 (and this is a point that should be of immense encouragement to John's believers), the testimony of previous witnesses had already helped to do before what their witness can and will do now.

Read this through the lens of slave owners in the American South. Like their corresponding Roman overlords at the end of the first century, they had all the power. They had all the resources. And yet they feared the worship of collected slaves and the running away of individual ones. Why? Because those acts were in themselves testimonials to a mythical truth that was in direct opposition to present historical fact. Clandestine worship services that pleaded for God's timely intervention and the public escapes that pointed a way to a world free from slavery encouraged hope in the slaves and at the same time weakened ideological and physical support for the system of slavery itself. Slave owners therefore feared a set of circumstances that, while nettlesome and disruptive, shouldn't have been feared at all. Why fear a gathering of slaves singing and praying to God in the dark of the night? Why fear the loss of one runaway when you could acquire or produce another to take his place? Why fear the dissemination of a silly myth that presented Christ as historical Lord?

John's time line is a provocative one. When chapter 12 opens, the dragon is in heaven. Not yet cast down to pursue the metaphorical church, it accuses the children from its legal position in heaven. These witnesses to God's justice and mercy apparently fare poorly before this heavenly prosecutor. If indeed the child's birth and snatching up to the throne of God is a symbolic representation of Jesus' death and resurrection, which provide God's ultimate victory over the power of death that the dragon represents, then this earthly victory coincides with the victory of Michael and the angels in heaven.[72] It is only at this point, after this victory, that the dragon is thrown down to pursue the people of God on the earth. But this is where the victory hymn takes place. Right here, at the point of that initial defeat. It interprets *that* defeat. And it connects that defeat to Jesus' death by specifically relating victory to the blood of the Lamb, who, because this is flashback, we now know is Jesus, the Christ. The dragon, representing Satan, was defeated by the blood of the Lamb, which we have already tied directly to the witness of Jesus on the cross.

John goes on to say that they—the believers whom he connects with the souls of 6:9–11 and 20:4—also conquered by the word of their witness. By this witness to Jesus' lordship, the same truth to which Jesus himself witnessed, they helped drive Satan out of heaven. This is an astounding claim. Yet it is the cosmic truth upon which they can depend and have hope. They know now what this witness can do. If their witness helped bring down Satan, surely it can help overturn the claims of historical lordship made by Rome.

The heavenly response is just as telling; it is an assurance that the work of witnessing will be completed by future "souls" who are their brothers and sisters. What must be encouraging at this point is not the realization that more believers will die, but that more believers will fulfill the witness that will transform human history, just as it once transformed cosmic reality. God's justice will come on earth, just as it came in heaven, and their witness will play a vital part. At 20:4 John narrates the confirmation.

John's flashing back to an earlier time to give hope in a present time is not unlike what presently happens in the Black Church tradition. Decades after the encouraging victories of the civil rights movement, battles against racial prejudice and injustice continue. Even now African Americans cry out the proverbial, "How long?"

Many a black preacher assures his or her congregation about God's coming justice by flashing back to the images of struggle and witness that helped God transform American society and put it on its proper track toward full racial equality. The realization of what *did* happen gives hope and assurance that full equality one day *will* happen. This seems precisely to be John's message at Revelation 12:10–12.

The second thing 12:10–12 provides is ethical exhortation. As Dorothy Lee points out, mythical reflections often have this-worldly objectives for guiding human behavior. "Reading the narrative [of chapter 12] in its sociocultural setting, this cosmic myth functions as 'parenesis'—that is, moral encouragement and motivation—for a hard pressed community."[73] Pablo Richard agrees: "Myths, and the visions that appear in myths, serve not only for contemplation, but are primarily for taking action. Myth expresses a fundamental conviction and transmutes a special energy for acting and for transforming history."[74] And if, as Revelation 12 seems to claim, our witness takes its shape and demeanor from Jesus' own witness, then its ethics can only be one of active confrontation. Boesak is clear:

> Jesus came, not simply to pour oil on our wounds or cover up the sinfulness of the world. He came to destroy the works of Satan. He did this not by matching the power of Satan with equal power; not with propaganda or violence; nor with the simple, pietistic sentimentality of the sweet, gentle Jesus invented by Western Christianity. He did it by his incarnation, his identification with the poor, the meek, and the lowly; by his engagement in the struggle for God's kingdom of shalom and justice and love, even at the price of his life.[75]

Operating from the oppressive context of South African apartheid, which too often mimicked the hostile realities John narrated about Rome, Boesak goes on to declare that our witness must therefore be a witness of resistance too: "First, there is a war on; there is a struggle. There is a fight for justice, peace, freedom, and reconciliation. These are not things that come to us on the wheels of inevitability. They must be fought for."[76] Myths, like those in Revelation 12, encourage just this kind of historical behavior. This is not surprising for those who live within the context of the Black Church tradition. For them, this way of reading myth has always been so. As Pinn puts it: "These [black] churches recognize a divine motivation for their activities in that the word of God requires spiritual and material freedom."[77] So also does the story of God, no matter how mythologically it is told.

Can I Get a Witness?

In *The Social Teaching of the Black Churches* Peter Paris writes that "the 'new breed' of scholars has been diligently demonstrating that blacks have functioned in every historical period as agents of change in spite of the extreme environmental constraints put upon them."[78] In other words, no matter what the circumstances, black folk have always believed that they could somehow find a transformative witness. John seems to believe it, too. That is why he chronicles events in the way that he does. He tells the story of past slaughtered, though heroic souls because he wants his hearers and readers to emulate them. He wants them to become witnesses too. His visionary call is not unlike the poetic call issued forth in the old African American spiritual "Witness," which, in chronicling the stories of valiant witnesses of past biblical tradition, hopes to provoke the probability for witness now. What was past can be present and future. The witness that once helped change the world can do so again. If, that is, we act it out. And that is why the slaves sang:

> My soul is a witness for my Lord,
> My soul is a witness for my Lord,
> My soul is a witness for my Lord,
> My soul is a witness for my Lord.

> You read in de Bible an' you understan',
> Metuselah was de oldes' man,
> He lived nine hundred an' sixty nine,
> He died an' went to Heav'n, Lord, in a-due time.

O, Metuselah was a witness for my Lord,
Metuselah was a witness for my Lord,
Metuselah was a witness for my Lord,
Metuselah was a witness for my Lord.

You read in de Bible and you understan',
Samson was de strongest man;
Samson went out at-a one time,
An' he killed about a thousan' of de Philistine.

Delilah fooled Samson, dis-a we know,
For de Holy Bible tells us so,
She shaved off his head jus' as clean as yo' han',
An' his strength became de same as any natch'-al man.

O, Samson was a witness for my Lord,
Samson was a witness for my Lord,
Samson was a witness for my Lord,
Samson was a witness for my Lord.

Now, Daniel was a Hebrew child,
He went to pray his God a-while,
De king at once for Daniel did sen',
An' he put him right down in de lions' den;
God sent His angels de lions for to keep,
An' Daniel laid down an' went to sleep.

Now, Daniel was a witness for my Lord,
Daniel was a witness for my Lord,
Daniel was a witness for my Lord,
Daniel was a witness for my Lord.

O, who'll be a witness for my Lord?
O, who'll be a witness for my Lord?
My soul is a witness for my Lord,
My soul is a witness for my Lord.[79]

Chapter 3

Wreaking Weakness:
The Way of the Lamb

When you throw weakness around, worlds change. Empires fall. Justice rises. People get hurt. Even, perhaps especially, the people who make the changes happen.

John's visionary thesis is that God shot Satan out of the sky and even now tracks him across the human, historical landscape in the crosshairs of the ultimate weapon, the slaughtered remains of his own Son. Seeking refuge behind the impersonation of a bestial Roman Empire, the draconian devil believes it has found a way to return fire against God by establishing on earth the lordship it could not claim in heaven. The power of countless legions at its back, the partnership of all the kings of the earth by its side, the wealth of the world's economy in its pocket, the rearmed adversary has ignited a conflict it is certain it has all the necessary strength to win.

God comes forward weakly. A dedicated child whom God apparently sacrificed to the war effort and has ghoulishly revived in the form of a defenseless, mangled Lamb goes out before his father on the point. A brood of unarmed, inexplicably impudent humans trails them. When the battle engages, the satanic master of misdirection wheels around to the rear flank and goes after God's flock instead. If it can destroy them, it can destroy God's presence and God's dominance on earth. First, it has to draw them out. It dares God's people to declare their allegiance to God's Son. When they do, it unleashes a deadly barrage of property theft, destruction of social standing, economic exploitation, and even execution. God fights back by exposing God's people in the same way that God had once exposed God's Son. On the cross. Naked and defenseless. Like a lamb led to the slaughter. And yet, unbelievably, God apparently believes this strategy will win the eternal day and transform human history into a reality in which the dragon is dead and God dwells directly and securely with God's people. According to John, God's victorious way is the slaughtered way; it not only *de*scribes the path God's Son took, it *pre*scribes the path God's people *will take* on their way to the new heaven and new earth their combative effort will help God create. They too are a vital part of God's arsenal; God will use their weakness the way the child David used a single one of his five smooth stones—to put the monster down.

All this battle imagery sounds a bit disconcerting. It is, however, John's imagery. For John, weakness is the silver bullet that God fires out like a deadeye marksman against the scarcely exposed heart of cosmic and human evil. For John, weakness is a weapon. Jesus deployed it on the cross; Jesus' followers must now trigger it with their lives.

Notice how John draws the connections. First, especially early on, when he is introducing the figure, John provocatively pairs *Lamb* with the adjective *slaughtered* (5:6, 8–9,12; 13:8).[1] The imagery brings to mind the *Tamid*, the ritual sacrifice that opened and ended the cultic day at the Temple in Jerusalem. Jesus' death on the cross is likened through the use of this imagery to the *Tamid* lamb, its throat cut, its blood drained out, its carcass hung on a hook. One cannot get much weaker than that.

But this is precisely when John makes an even more daring move. He aligns this startling snapshot of perennial shortcoming, the slaughtered Lamb, with what might well be the most complete symbol of utmost power, the heavenly throne. Of the eighteen combat-oriented circumstances in which John uses the Lamb, half occur either with or in direct proximity to the mention of God's throne (5:6, 8, 9, 12, 13; 6:1,16; 7:9, 10, 14, 17; 12:11; 13:8, 11; 14:1, 4, 10; 15:3; 17:14.[2] For John, literarily at least, *slaughtered* equals power.[3] The complete formulation, *slaughtered Lamb*, operates for John the way parables operated for Jesus, taking on qualities people expect, then overturning them. All of a sudden, Jesus' status as victim morphs into that of victor. It is as if the Lamb, acting exactly the way one expects a Lamb to act, or, in this case, to be acted upon, produces like a lion.

How do we know? By the way John depicts the end of his Lamb narration. The final nine occurrences, the last two of which are also directly linked to the heavenly throne, depict the wedding imagery of a victorious Lamb and the revolutionary heaven and new earth he has championed.[4] Though I do not want to deal with that transformation as much as with the methodology the Lamb used to establish it, it is clear that for John a transformation does occur. It occurs because of the Lamb and the people who follow in his "slaughtered" way. It is that way, as John depicts it, that I would like to consider.

The Lamb as Suffering Sacrifice

In the typical Christian view, the slaughtered lamb is lit up like a blinking, neon sign that marks God's strategy as one of redemptive suffering and sacrifice. Jesus is, in other words, the quintessential martyr, the man who surrenders his innocent life so that others, even the guilty, may go free. In this atonement-oriented reading of John's Apocalypse (see 1:5), Satan was owed his due for crimes God's people had committed against God and each other. Cosmic law was exact and unyielding; human sin warranted capital punishment. Someone had to pay: humankind or someone standing in its place. To save humanity, God chose the latter option. God paid the price by giving up God's Son to Satan's legalistic demands, thereby breaking Satan's hold over humanity and setting it free. Jesus' death on the cross, mythically described by John at 12:5 as the snatching of a messianic son to the throne of heaven, erased the debt. That "snatching," though, is precisely the problem. In the end, God cheats death by reclaiming the Son's life. Satan therefore loses both its claim over humanity and its divine kill. No longer able to accuse a graciously exonerated humankind of sinfulness, the adversary even loses its heavenly position. Thrown down, it is thrown out of cosmic power.

Infuriated, dragonlike in its form and method of operation, it now roams the earth directly engaging the humans that it could attack before only from a heavenly distance. This time God enlists those who trust in the sacrifice of God's Son to counterattack. God commands them to fight the way the Son fought; his way will be their way. This is why it is crucial to determine precisely what that way is. If Jesus did accomplish his task by suffering and dying redemptively for others, his followers must suffer and die redemptively as well.[5] The way of sacrificial slaughter will be their way of discipleship.

At first sight, there appears to be a happy correspondence between this traditional way of viewing Jesus as a slaughtered, sacrificed Lamb and the suffering circumstance that surrounds the Black Church tradition in the United States. The appearance is deceptive. As JoAnne Marie Terrell points out, in introducing African slaves to Christianity, American evangelicalism imposed a standard of piety that "urged slaves to imitate Christ substantively, through personal sacrifice as their bounden duty."[6] Pinn agrees: In their "Christian" examination of the problem of suffering and evil, black slaves reached two primary conclusions: (1) unmerited suffering is evil, but can have redemptive consequences; (2) God and humans are coworkers in the struggle to remove evil.[7]

The problem is that slaves came to believe through white teaching and their own internalization of white spirituality that *their* unmerited suffering was God's chosen tactic for effecting that removal. The end result was a spiritualization of Jesus' suffering and death that mandated that slaves similarly surrender their own lives for others. The role of the "others" was too often wickedly played by slave owners. The end result was a hermeneutic of sacrifice. It ignored the injustice of the slave condition; it praised instead the slave who, because of his or her love for the Lord, forfeited his or her entire life and work effort to the demands the slave condition imposed. Terrell argues, "Through brute force, paternalistic compromise and the hermeneutics of sacrifice, European Americans called upon African Americans to surrender their labor, their agency and, perhaps most critically, their identity."[8] In the ultimate stratagem of "No pain, no gain," suffering through the slave condition became a small price to pay for the God-willed opportunity that slavery itself made possible: knowledge of Christ in this life that would surely lead to an existence with Christ in eternity. A few lines from the young black slave poet Phyllis Wheatley makes the point:

> 'Twas mercy brought me from my Pagan land,
> Taught my benighted soul to understand
> That there's a God, that there's a Saviour too:
> Once I redemption neither sought nor knew.
> Some view our sable race with scornful eye
> "Their colour is a diabolic die."
> Remember, Christians, Negros, black as Cain,
> May be refin'd, and join th' angelic train.[9]

Terrell argues that this hermeneutic of sacrifice led to the deradicalization of the Black Church in the period following Reconstruction and on into the Jim Crow era. The church was so desperately focused on spiritual salvation and the identification of its own struggles with the redemptive crucifixion of Christ that it either dismissed or accommodated itself and its communicants to the savageries of racist separatism and hate.[10] Properly understood, suffering was rehabilitative and redemptive; it shored up a believer's faith while it solicited God's salvific intervention. The faithful believer ought therefore to endure it heroically, even thankfully. Pinn believes that the effect of this hermeneutic still drives the church today. How else to interpret the constant prayer refrains of suffering sisters and mothers in his foundational AME churches? "The words of Sunday morning prayers have stayed with me: 'Lord, you never said it would be easy . . . and so, if I'm going to wear a crown, I must bear my cross."[11]

The only problem, Pinn cautions, is that "bearing one's cross" never brings about the liberative transformation it promises:

> I argue that the history of Black religious thought on suffering—Black "theodicy"—makes clear the dominance and unacceptability of redemptive suffering arguments. These arguments are unacceptable because they counteract efforts

at liberation by finding something of value in Black suffering. In essence such arguments go against social transformation activity. Redemptive suffering and liberation are
diametrically opposed ideas; they suggest ways of being in
the world that, in effect, nullify each other.[12]

What, then, does one do with the slaughtered Lamb of the
Apocalypse? Revelation intends social, political, and historical
transformation; the oracle of the new heaven and a new earth testify to that. Revelation also intends that human disciples in some
way participate in the construction of this realization (12:11). But
if suffering is always evil and ultimately self-defeating, can the
slaughtered Lamb remain a positive role-model image? Can a
more sophisticated constituency of Black Church believers, who
recognize a call to suffer for the deceptive and evil ruse that it is,
find transformative hope in John's shockingly traumatic Christ
symbol? What can a slaughtered Lamb do for a perennially suffering people?

According to Terrell, this is precisely the question being asked
by womanist theologians. "Black women, too, have begun to question Christian sacrificial tradition: does the image of Jesus as surrogate figure have salvific power for black women, or does it
reinforce the exploitation that accompanies their experience of
surrogacy? . . . In other words, is the profession of faith in the cross
inimical to black women's self-interests? Or, is there power in the
blood?"[13]

There is no doubt that John sees power in the slaughtered
Lamb and his blood.[14] But what are black women, consumed by a
tridimensional reality of racist, classist, and sexist suffering, to do
with a redeemer whose primary features are visceral wounds that
encourage a brand of discipleship that will likewise lacerate his
followers? Not much, if Terrell is right.

With feminist theologians, womanist theologians have
recently identified the motif of Christ's surrogacy (on which
hinge traditional theories of the Atonement) as problematic
in the confession of faith not only because of its utility in

sanctioning women's oppression but also because of its similarity to the historical conscription of black women in surrogate roles in relationship to white men, white women and their children. Moreover, black women have historically been obliged to be surrogates for black men.[15]

To be sure, Pinn and Terrell do not represent all of the Black Church tradition, and they should not be compelled, as so many black scholars are, to speak for their race. But they are a scholarly *part* of the Black Church tradition that seems to fall broadly in line with a critical component of John's theological perspective. John also appears to view unearned suffering as an evil (6:9–11). And John, though he does call the Lamb "slaughtered," depicts him as anything but sacrificial (5:5; 19:11–16). How could John reject unearned, sacrificial suffering, but simultaneously symbolize his protagonist as a slaughtered Lamb? If the slaughter does not stick (he is, after all, still standing), why keep using it? Since Pinn and Terrell witness to the same struggle in the Black Church, I wonder whether reading the Apocalypse through their eyes might prove helpful in clarifying its narrative intent.

Clearly, at least according to them, continuing to view the slaughtered Lamb through the traditional black religious lens of redemptive suffering is not the answer. What is? Pinn, walking out of and away from the Black Church, argues for humanism. Though the mere word conjures fear and trembling in most Black Church traditionalists, Pinn professes that it has long been a part of the black religious tradition, although he concedes that the Black Church is dominated by weak humanist thinking.[16] "This position argues for the questioning of God's power in the world and declares that humans must not depend upon God for liberation; they must work *with* God to achieve this goal."[17] He contends that leaders like Martin Luther King Jr. and academics like James Cone have professed just such a view, but its problem is this: "Weak humanism is in keeping with Black Church tradition and does not avoid the 'theodical pothole' of redemptive suffering."[18] Weak humanism cannot explain how a good and omnipotent God allows suffering unless it declares that suffering to be somehow redemptive, somehow "good," somehow at least partially responsible for the liberative endeavor humans working with God can achieve. Strong humanism avoids that trap. Having rid itself of the premise of God, it is free to place the focus where it belongs, on human beings.

> This form of humanism understands suffering as wrong and sees it as being solely a result of human misconduct. Suffering is evil and it must end; contact with it and endurance of it do not promote anything beneficial. To think otherwise is to deny the value of human life by embracing a demonic force that effectively mutates and destroys the quality of life. *Suffering has no redemptive qualities.*[19]

Well, what about a suffering, slaughtered, messianic Lamb? According to Pinn's way of thinking, one must either jettison the symbol or, at the very least, read it through a strong humanist lens. That is not completely unthinkable. After all, the souls crying furiously under the heavenly altar (6:9–11) apparently feel as much distaste for human suffering as Pinn does. After all, when the Lamb finally makes his move to help them, he doesn't climb back upon the cross, he mounts a war horse and unsheathes a sword (19:11–16). He is about to change the world, not suffer for it.

In the end, though, the strong humanist lens cannot fit. The Lamb, after all, takes to the battlefield with God's word as his primary weapon. The Lamb also remains God's Son. One cannot read Revelation without reading God into the narrative. One might even say the same thing about African American history. Humanistic attempts to provide a transformative alternative to black misery have proved as problematic as those founded upon the platform of redemptive suffering. Terrell highlights the Deist fallacy. It "permitted the ongoing enslavement of African people, not only because it denied the providence of God—and hence, the *sovereignty* of God over human, temporal matters—but also because it elevated one group of humans at the expense of another."[20]

There is no guarantee that, simply because one holds human beings solely accountable for human suffering and applies human reason to the curtailment of that suffering, the suffering circumstance will be transformed. There is also no reason to believe Pinn's reverse premise that belief in God cripples the fight for social change. He asks, somewhat cynically, "How strongly does one fight for change while seeking signs of God's presence?"[21] One might refer that question to African American Christians like Denmark Vesey, Nat Turner, Harriet Tubman, and Martin Luther King Jr. While agreeing with and absorbing Pinn's challenge that we should never valorize human suffering, I prefer to read the slaughtered Lamb with and through those African American leaders.

We must also add the clarifying focus of the womanist lens. Womanist theologians rebut the hermeneutic of sacrifice by shifting the focus from Jesus' suffering to Jesus' life and ministry, and by observing that it was the work that Jesus performed in that ministry that accomplished the transformation of the relationship between God and humans. His suffering and death were never God's goal; they were, as Pinn might point out, the sole consequence of human (mis)behavior. It is not surprising that those who benefited from a society structured around the aristocratic few would target for destruction a social transformer of Jesus' capability and following. This is why Delores Williams argues that the cross and Jesus' crucifixion upon it "are reminders of what can happen to reformers who successfully challenge the status quo and try to bring about a new dispensation of love and power for the poor."[22] They are a warning that a life committed to social transformation will entail struggle and perhaps even great suffering. They are not, however, a call to suffer. Through this womanist reading lens, then, hearers and readers of John's Revelation are directed behind the Lamb's slaughter to the ministry that led up to it and was responsible for it. The narrative itself will tell us whether this is the reading it ultimately prefers.

At this point the work of Loren Johns becomes particularly helpful. A New Testament interpreter, Johns focuses exclusively on what he calls the rhetorical force of the Lamb symbolism in the Apocalypse. He asks a pertinent question: how, in their particular social-historical setting, did John's readers appropriate his Lamb language? After an exhaustive survey of lamb imagery in early

Judaism, he concludes that "there is no evidence at this point to establish the existence of anything like a recognizable redeemer-lamb figure in [its] apocalyptic traditions."[23] John would therefore not have expected his readers to connect his lamb's suffering/slaughter to their own redemption. A survey of the Hebrew Bible affords no better warrant. In a study that offers the most relevance for our particular concern about the redemptive efficacy of the Lamb's slaughter, Johns explicitly rules out a transformative suffering agenda. After comparing texts that discussed lambs used for sin atonement with the lamb language in Revelation, he concludes, "the terminology used in the Apocalypse does not fit well with the lambs of the sacrificial system."[24] In fact, he points out appropriately that John does not even restrict slaughter language to the Lamb (see 6:4, 9; 13:3; 18:24). His conclusion: "In none of these other cases is the 'slaughter' considered expiatory, reducing the possibility that the rhetorical force of the 'slaughter' of the Lamb in 5:6 is primarily expiatory."[25] He then broadens his conclusion even further. Given that only one hymn (1:5–6) has even any remote expiatory themes connected to it, and given that this hymn occurs well outside the central section of the conflict visions (chapters 4–19), he argues that "there is little in the Apocalypse of John to support this understanding of Jesus' death as Atonement."[26]

Pinn and Terrell would no doubt be delighted. Their theological concerns apparently jibe with the narrative's intent; John does not highlight the Lamb as slaughtered in order to valorize his suffering. According to Johns, the seer is showcasing his vulnerability and nonviolent resistance instead.[27] In yet another exhaustive survey, he tracks the symbolic use of *lamb* in the Old Testament. He finds that, while in a few cases it denotes victimization by either God or humans, "vulnerability *without* victimization seems precisely to be the sign of the eschaton: the passages that treat lambs as symbols in the visions of eschatological peace portray vulnerable lambs as safe in the presence of their traditional predators."[28]

And yet, as Johns and everyone else who reads Revelation notices, John's resistant Lamb is hardly a vulnerable figure. He is a conquering lion (5:5), armed with the fullness of God's power (symbolized by the seven horns, 5:6), who deposes the dragon Satan

(12:11), and, having taken up the sword of God's word, rides out to meet Satan's forces on the field of apocalyptic battle (2:16; 19:11–16). How is one to hold these opposite dramatizations of vulnerability and conquest together in a believable narrative tension?

The Lamb as Homeopathic Cure

To help answer that question, I turn to the work of another interpreter of the Black Church tradition, Theophus Smith. Like Pinn, Smith broadens the horizons of the Black Church tradition. He includes within its theoretical compass the phenomenon of African conjure that crossed the Atlantic with the slaves and syncretistically embedded itself within the traditions of African American Christianity. He is particularly intrigued by the conjure concept of the homeopathic cure. In effecting a "cure," the conjuror takes an obvious negative and reconstitutes it into something positive and efficacious. By way of example, Smith offers the name change of former slave Isabella Baumfree upon her release in 1827. When she gave herself the name Sojourner Truth, she initiated an "existential transformation similar to that of the young Saul in 1 Samuel 10.6."[29] Her effort was therapeutic; it remedied the perception that she was an inferior being owned by and therefore needing to be named by someone else. It was also homeopathic in that "it mimicked the 'diseased situation' of racist cognitive perceptions, precisely in order to counter those perceptions and to cure that disease."[30] Truth laid claim to the warped principles of African American naming, whereby a slave owner conveyed identity with the issuance of a name, and reconfigured them. She took that prerogative upon herself. The new name conveyed a new purchase. For Freedom.

John is such a conjuror. Right before our disoriented eyes, he transfigures a slaughtered Lamb into a conquering Lion without surrendering either its homicide or its helplessness. It is a homeopathic act.

How does he do it? He operates the way every good conjuror operates; he creates an effective antidote by capturing a small dose of the disease, reprogramming it, and then turning it back on itself. In Smith's words, "a mimetic form of a disease is prescribed to cure that disease."[31] Or, to work within the dragon characterization that John so ably employs, homeopathic cure is like stirring the milked venom of a poisonous snake into the bowl of ingredients that, when fully cooked, will neutralize the toxin injected by the serpent's fangs. To use yet another of Smith's illustrations, "In the signal case of immunization, the intention is to mimic the disease in a manner that skillfully engages the body's natural defenses without allowing the disease a full range of operation."[32] African Americans have been as skilled at applying this homeopathic principle to their social situation as physicians have been at applying it to their battles with biological disease. Black music is a notable case in point: "the blues mode of transformation, in which one counteracts a melancholy mood by means of a melancholy tune, is homologous, or similar in function, to conjurational practices which are homeopathic in nature."[33]

In the book of Revelation, John captures a dose of violence, the slaughter of the Lamb, and homeopathically reconfigures it into the one weapon capable of tearing violence apart. To be sure, it is a theological high-wire act of the trickiest sort. Using violence to conquer violence is an age-old, centuries-tested recipe for failure; for violence, in no matter how small or how carefully apportioned a dosage, tends more toward replication than cure. Depending heavily upon the work of René Girard, Smith analyzes how some societies have attempted to solve this conundrum.[34] Leaders on opposing sides of a hostility attempt to contain an outbreak of all-out violence, wherein huge segments of a population or different populations square off against each other, by directing necessary blame for the conflict at a single individual or group of individuals—the scapegoat. Each side holds this scapegoat responsible for the outbreak of hostility. Because the scapegoat takes the blame, it must also pay the price. Theoretically, the violence unleashed against the scapegoat should appease the will to violence by both embattled sides. This is how sacrifice works; it is a homeopathic attempt to use a small dose of violence, directed against some sacrificial victim, either to preempt or to conclude an episode of divine or human fury. This is how many Christians read the slaughtered "sacrificial" Lamb of Revelation. The Lamb was violently sacrificed upon the cross in order to appease Satan's desire for humanity's destruction and God's need for humanity's judgment. Either of those eventualities would have brought about violent cataclysms on an apocalyptic scale.

In this way of thinking, John calls upon the slaughtered Lamb as a way of reminding his hearers and readers how God contained the destructive violence they deserved and then graciously accepted them. They were refined because somebody else, the Lamb, voluntarily went into their fire. Now, though, it is their turn. In order to complete the transformation, they must now become the sacrificial scapegoat; they must mimic their model. When sufficient violence has been brought against them (cf. 6:11), God will initiate the judgment that will destroy their enemies and transform their violent history into a tranquil new heaven and a peaceful new earth.

The problem with this very traditional reading of the Lamb and his followers is that, as Johns' work has pointed out, Revelation's language does not support a sacrificial, scapegoat interpretation of the slaughtered Lamb.[35] If the Lamb is not a sacrificial scapegoat, then surely neither are the hearers and readers whom John asks to be witnesses and followers of the Lamb. What, then, is the slaughtered Lamb? He is a dosage of violence that is not only quantitatively reconfigured into a lesser amount, but is also qualitatively transfigured into a different substance. In his characterization as slaughtered, nonviolence is extracted from violence and then set out as an antidote against it.

Consider the witness discussion in chapter 2. There I made the case that in presenting Jesus as the ultimate witness, John refers back to Jesus' testimony to his own lordship on the cross. Jesus engaged the rulers of his day; but he did so with his word. He did so nonviolently. Womanist interpreters, as we have seen, wouldn't stop there. They would point back to the witness of Jesus' entire ministry, a nonviolent witness that sought to transform human life by engaging and resisting oppressive forces through a healing, teaching, and exorcising ministry. Smith reads the Gospel accounts of Jesus' ministry similarly and puts it into his own therapeutic language: "Over against a cure of violence which generates culture by-means-of-violence, the gospels aim to regenerate culture on the basis of a salvific will—the will to save or 'make well.'"[36] But is that the real background and foreground of the Apocalypse? Johns seems to think so: "The lamb is strong, but the exhibition of its strength is unconventional: its strength lies in its consistent, nonviolent resistance to evil—a resistance that led to its execution."[37] John himself mimics the Lamb's activity by also witnessing in a costly, but yet nonviolent way. "According to Revelation 1:9, John shares in that witness even though he has not himself yet been killed. This point is important because it shows that the 'witness' envisioned in the Apocalypse is not just a 'passive acceptance of suffering . . . but rather the sort of nonviolent resistance to evil in which both Jesus and John engaged."[38]

"Nonviolent?" some critics mutter. What about all the bloodletting that takes place throughout the book? It doesn't take much more than a surface reading to recognize that the Lamb is indeed noted for *being* slaughtered, not for slaughtering others. Even at 19:11–16, when John says that he judges and makes war, and thus rides out onto the battlefield in a robe dipped in blood, the Lamb never actually fights. Battle is never engaged. The blood on his robe is his own; he does, after all, still bear the residue of slaughter. His offensive weapon is a sharp sword, but it is clearly tied to his identity as the word of God. He issues it sharply from his mouth (1:16; 2:16; 19:15); when it cuts, it does so cleanly against the contrary witness that Rome and Caesar are Lord. The sure implication is that the sword of Jesus' mouth is his cutting testimony of his own true lordship. It represents oppositional witness, not violent combat.

Because of this witness, the Lamb is slaughtered. And yet, in John's conjured, symbolic universe, that slaughter does not make him a sacrificial victim. There are several reasons why not. First, by presenting the slaughtered Lamb as still standing, John conjures even death. As Johns puts it, "Essential to a proper understanding of the book's rhetoric is the recognition that the lamb *has triumphed in* his death and resurrection."[39] In the combat mythology of chapter 12, at the legendary point of presumable death on the cross, the Lamb is snatched away from the dragon's grip and installed at the seat of God's heavenly power. John seizes a small dosage of fatality and with it converts death into eternal, omnipotent life.

Second, this lamb is no innocent; he *earns* the slaughter that comes his way. To be sure, this is an odd thing to say. And yet it is an accurate representation of both John's Apocalypse and some of the key transformative moments in the history of the Black Church tradition. Smith offers the work of Martin Luther King Jr. as a primary example. "This new feature of the King phenomenon was the crafting of homeopathic performances in which a sufficiently small instance of a social disorder is rendered efficacious for exposing and (thereby) countering that disorder."[40] By deploying a small amount of nonviolent resistance, King drew out the reactionary violence of racial injustice and transformed it. When a shocked U.S. and global population witnessed the horrible violence unleashed against the nonviolent protesters, the very Lamblike wrath of their outrage rained down in the form of executive, legislative, judicial, and martial intervention and reform. One can say that the civil rights protesters who were beaten, water hosed, bombed, threatened, tortured, and even killed were, like the Lamb, slaughtered. But one would not properly call them victims, even if their victory did come at what were often tragic costs. At the very moment their oppressors executed their violence against them, the moment of their symbolic "slaughter," their battle was won.

Pinn is not so sure. He interprets King's actions as those of a man intoxicated by the false promise of sacrificial, redemptive suffering. He quotes King's own words to make the point:

> As victories for civil rights mount in the federal courts, the angry poison and deep prejudices . . . will be further aroused. These persons will do all within their power to provoke us and make us angry. But we must not retaliate with external physical violence or internal violence of spirit . . . As we continue the struggle for our own freedom we will be persecuted, abused and called bad names. But we must go with the faith that unearned suffering is redemptive, and love is the most durable power in all the world.[41]

The key here is one's interpretation of the adjective *unearned*. Pinn took it to mean sacrificial victimization. While it is clear that no one who fights for justice and equality deserves the hostility that often comes, I would argue for a broader interpretation. King appears to mean that he and the civil rights activists who followed him, because their cause was just, did not *deserve* the suffering that came their way. They were just and appropriate witnesses to the equality of African Americans. However, they did not exist in a just and appropriate circumstance. In a hostile Jim Crow environment, where segregation was backed up by the force of municipal, state, and federal law, they stood up and witnessed to a contrary truth. In that sense, they "earned" the retaliatory, reactionary response they received, even though they did not *deserve* it. Those sitting in at a segregated lunch counter or defiantly plopping themselves down in the front of a bus when they had been legally consigned to the back will "earn" the abuse they receive. Just as John "earned" his exile. Just as Antipas "earned" his death (2:14). Just as the Lamb "earned" his slaughter. Just as the followers of the Lamb who dare to stand up and witness to a truth that contradicts the declared truth of municipal, state, and imperial power will "earn" theirs. These are not sacrificial victims; these are fully engaged, nonviolent, activist witnesses.

Once again Pinn quotes King to chastise him for valorizing suffering. Once again, I believe he misreads him.

> As my sufferings mounted I soon realized that there were two ways that I could respond to my situation: either to react with bitterness or seek to transform the suffering into a creative force . . . Recognizing the necessity for suffering I have tried to make of it a virtue. If only to save myself from bitterness, I have attempted to see my personal ordeals as an opportunity to transform myself and heal the people involved in the tragic situation which now obtains.[42]

Clearly King attempts here to conjure suffering into a therapeutic cure. Recognizing the necessity of suffering, though, is not necessarily the same thing as valorizing it. What is the necessity of suffering for King? Really, there is none. Had he retreated from the cause, "just gone somewhere and sat down," the suffering he endured would not only have been unnecessary, it would have disappeared. The suffering the civil rights activists endured was not necessary in the sense that it was divinely ordained; it was necessary in the sense that many powerful people and forces in the South so wanted to maintain segregation that they could be counted upon to use force against anyone acting to disrupt it. Suffering was not King's goal in any case. His goal was the transformation of an oppressive social situation. He was, however, willing to endure the suffering his activist behavior "earned," in order to bring that transformation about. Even Pinn himself recognizes the plausibility of such an interpretation when he begrudgingly includes a clarifying King quote: "Suffering in itself is not redemptive nor is it ordained by God; rather, it is contrary to Christian principles of unity and proper behavior."[43] Undeserved, suffering is often well "earned." Not in a sacrificial or redemptive sense, but in a transforming, conjuring one.

Third, John's slaughtered Lamb is not a sacrificial victim because his homeopathic cure is an intentional display of aggressive, one might even say predatory, power. Smith makes his point again using the civil rights ministry of King; the homeopathy of nonviolence is still a will-to-power. In fact, this is why Smith studies King. "I investigate King's religious heritage for its power simultaneously to overturn ethnic victimization and to transform the victimizer—for its *power* to realize what he called 'the beloved community.'"[44] On this point, Pinn agrees, seeing how King—particularly in his later years (a point James Cone makes in more detail in his fine work on King and Malcolm X[45])—recognizes the importance of power in any transformational dynamic:

> In later years (1962–68), King recognized that the inhumanity of white Americans toward Black Americans was more systemic than he initially realized. As a result, King shifted his emphasis away from love (and moral persuasion) as the counterbalance of dwarfed moral conscience to justice (and "nonviolent coercion") as the demand of love. Hence, love

had to be combined with acquired power and full participation in a reformed love.[46]

King himself was quite specific: "Power without love is reckless and abusive and . . . love without power is sentimental and anemic."[47]
I believe that this emphasis on the necessity of power is the reason John finds it necessary, before he introduces Christ as the slaughtered Lamb, to announce him as a mighty Lion (5:5). There is every narrative indication that John thinks the two titles belong together. In the end, neither subverts the other. The Lion reveals a Lamb; the Lamb remains a Lion. Patricia McDonald advises that John hints at his intention by the way he uses his language: "There is, on the whole, a distinction between what John sees and what he hears. . . . Hearing tends to give the inner reality of what is seen."[48] Perhaps it is no coincidence, then, that John *hears* the moniker *lion*, but *sees* a Lamb. Whenever the hearer/reader *sees* the Lamb in the remainder of the narrative, the staging of this chapter 5 character profile suggests that he or she *hear* the footsteps of a lurking Lion. Robert Mounce, after observing that John has retrofit this particular Lamb with the symbolism of perfect power (seven horns) and complete wisdom (seven eyes) agrees: "The *arnion* [lamb] of Revelation is not a dramatic contrast to the figure of the Lion but an extension of the same powerful figure."[49] The slaughtered Lamb is a powerful conqueror (5:5, 6; 12:11; 17:14). And yet there is something unique about this Lion/Lamb's modus operandi. "Although [John's] lion of Judah 'conquers' . . . it does so not in a lion-like way, by tearing its prey to pieces and devouring it, nor even in the military way that the imagery surely implies."[50] It conquers through predatory weakness.
Does this kind of description hold? It did for King. An observer of his nonviolent, active, engaged, and acerbic resistance would not have been wrong to describe him as a "Lion" for justice and equality. An observer of John's slaughtered Lamb could also describe the Lamb as a Lion. Perhaps this is precisely why, after his initial chapter 5 introduction, John no longer feels it necessary to continue the lion language. The hearer/reader no longer needs it; he or she has the slaughtered Lamb, which is the appropriate

narrative interpretation of the Lion. The slaughtered Lamb is *how* the Lion manifests himself in the world. In other words, the predatory way of the Lion *is* the slaughtered Lamb. *Slaughtered Lamb*, then, is not so much a descriptive, static noun as it is a paradoxical, action verb. Though John's Lion is a powerful conqueror, it would not be right to say that this Lion "*hunts* his prey." The more appropriate language would be something like, "this lion *slaughtered Lambs* (*sLambs*) his prey." This Lion *slaughtered Lambs* (*sLambs*) the dragon and the beasts that historically represent him.[51] The weak Lamb, then, does not subvert the powerful Lion; the Lamb's weakness, his slaughter, is precisely the way the Lion works out his power. The Lion *sLambs* God's opposition.

He does so on his own active, preemptive terms. Johns's survey of the social historical situation of the Apocalypse reveals a tantalizing interpretative clue. In a reconstruction that represents today's prevailing scholastic thinking, he argues that there was no wholesale persecution of Christians during Domitian's reign (81–96 CE), the time John was most likely writing. The evidence suggests that John was writing about the "*expectation* of persecution rather than the present *experience* of persecution."[52] The problem lay with the imminent conflict he knew would erupt if his hearers and readers lived out the kind of nonaccommodating Christianity that he himself professed. He was concerned primarily about the claims of lordship declared by Rome and Caesar and the witness to those claims made in the local municipalities where his churches were located. Johns paints a historical picture of local leaders pitched in feverish competition to land the rights to build temples praising the divinity of the emperor and the lordship of Rome. In order to fit in socially, politically, economically, and religiously in these communities, John's followers would have to accommodate themselves to the demands of these localized cultic affections. Resisting those demands would invite trouble.

Trouble, however, had apparently not yet arisen. That might well mean that John's believers were all too occupied in the business of accommodation. "The resistance called for was an *offensive* maneuver as John tried to unmask the spiritual powers at work behind the churches' compromising involvement in the empire, in its commerce, and in its imperial cult."[53] The fact that other Christian prophets, whom he calls Jezebel, the Nicolaitans, and Balaam, were approving of such behavior raised his hackles even further. John was unyielding; there could be no compromise with any activities that gave credence to the idea that Caesar, Rome, or Rome-sponsored divinities held title to the allegiance due only God and the Lamb.

But if all this is correct—if there was only sporadic persecution, if John's people were not vulnerably standing out because they were finding ways comfortably to blend in and accommodate— then the seer's immediate problem was, as Johns points out, more spiritual than social and historical. The social-historical crisis wouldn't arise *unless* John's people actually started to live by the mandates his apocalyptic prophecy demanded: "the resolution of that spiritual crisis would ironically induce a very real and dangerous *social* crisis as the churches began faithfully to resist the imperial cult and to face the consequences of their allegiance to Christ."[54]

This recognition is precisely what makes Lamblike behavior active and aggressive, even as it remains "weakly" nonviolent. If John was indeed asking his people to stand up and stand out in a world that they had accepted and that had accepted them, he was essentially telling them to go out and pick a fight! He was ordering them to go declare that they were now nonaccommodating Christians, who could no longer participate in a world that hadn't really noticed them because they had heretofore been accommodating to it. In a classic "don't ask, don't tell" (that I'm a Christian) kind of environment, John was essentially ordering his Christians to be about the business of telling on themselves, with full knowledge of the kind of repercussions such telling would bring. He was asking them to come screaming out of the Christian closet, knowing that it would solicit the same consequence it had attracted to the Lamb. Slaughter.

However, as we can plainly see, slaughter was *not* the goal. The goal was an active ministry of resistance that would witness to the singular lordship of Jesus Christ. Ironically, just as Jesus' death led to his empowered life, the slaughtering of John's readers would help lead to the transformative goal of eternal life in a new heaven and new earth where that lordship was on full display (12:10–12). This is how the homeopathic cure works. For those who are slaughtered because they stand up for Christ and therefore cause themselves to stand out to Rome and its Asian vassals, defeat is conjured to victory, oppression is conjured to liberation, death is conjured to life. Like death itself, the dragon and the imperial power that worships and represents it are *sLambed*.

Chapter 4

The Rap against Rome: The Spiritual-Blues Impulse and the Hymns of Revelation

The Symphony

I'm so sick, and tired of waitin, I'm wired
of non action and factions and these Romans.
All-reaction, no pro-action, this is taxing
I'm so tired and sick 1 through 6 was so thick
what comes now, interlude, it's so rude
my body is hurtin, I'm certain I'm hungry
need to eat, be complete, just the bread and the wine
just to dine at the table, I think that I'm able
to ingest, just a test, for this quest, I'm a mess.
Deaconess and deacons, the pastor and preachers
don't trust me to commune, static union
To prove of my worth and my right just by birth
I pause just to say, just to pray
Our father who art in heaven hallowed be thy name. Thy
   kingdom come thy will be done on earth as it is in heaven.
   As it is in heaven be done down on earth
I'm worthy I'm willing I'm waiting and wired
My assignment to eat, it tastes sweet but I'm weak, it turns
   out what I eat was a treat bittersweet.
I'm filled and I'm full, not a fool and not foul
take a towel and some soap it's so dope:

I'm on a world tour to prophesy with my man, not a mic but
  with a rod in my hand.
Learn the language and nation, meet the rulers, yes the rulers
  with my ruler to measure. Who's in VIP who's out 666 it's
  no trick
radio 1260 am are you out are you in
we spit fire, falls on you from above, for no love
I will bless them that bless you and curse them that curse you
we have power for an hour for a minute wait a minute
the beast is unleashed from the pit bottomless
we are ambushed, bamboozled; the beast makes a speech.
"We will war on them, conquer and kill them. 1 and 2 are no
  more. They are dead"
it's a trip like Egypt how bout Sodom don't forget
the one case of my Lord crucified and he died satisfied in the
  tomb, it turned out was his womb. 1 night 2 nights then
  day Christ who?
Lay dead in the street my heart has no beat
it's like woe, it's like woe CPR it's like woe
God's love from above, liberate, I awake.
The symphony plays triumphant for days
every day every hour of God's love of God's power

For Kirby Spivey III (Princeton Theological Seminary MDiv,
2001; ThM, 2002), a student charged with a classroom presentation on Revelation from the perspective of hip-hop culture, those
words, like the hymns of the Apocalypse that gave them inspira-
tion, personify the politics of worship. Music, like the provocative
Word of God to which it often responds, is a double-edged sword.
Some swear that it soothes. Others admit that it instigates, incites,
and ignites. Loren Johns makes the point: "Despite the success
Constantinian Christianity has enjoyed in schooling readers to see
[the language of Revelation] as 'spiritual,' the political critique
inherent in this language could hardly have been missed by first-
century readers. The language of kings, kingdoms, and reigning
(the *basil*-word group) abounds in this book."[1] More specifically
to the point, this kind of language abounds in its hymns.

There is more. The hymns sing what the rest of the book narratively declares. As Elisabeth Schüssler Fiorenza puts it, "Recent studies of the hymnic materials in Rev. have convincingly demonstrated that the hymns comment on and complement the visions and auditions of the book. Thus they function in the same way as the chorus in the Greek drama, preparing and commenting upon the dramatic movements of the plot."[2] I believe they function in the same way as the music of the Black Church tradition. Music is not a mere accompaniment to the liberative history of the Black Church tradition; it is the vital life force that paces the beating of its struggling, idealistic, weary, and yet indefatigable heart. If oppression has been one of the constant combatants threatening the existence of black folk in the United States, music has been a primary weapon black people have waged in their fighting back. The more I read the hymnic language in the Apocalypse through this lens, the more I am convinced that it does more than "prepare and comment upon" plot movements. It also reinforces the plot thesis of resistance while it incites John's hearers and readers to initiate such resistance in their own lives. The hymns pump up the volume of worship to a frenzy of praise that describes God as the Lord of all creation who will crack *down* on Rome while raising *up* the Lamb. In doing this, the hymns first capture the combustible emotions of fear, loss, anger, deprivation, and hope, and then set those emotions cultically and politically ablaze in a way that only the poetry and melody of music can.

The Lens: A Spiritual-Blues Impulse

Before reading Revelation's hymns through the musical lens of the Black Church tradition, I first must describe the lens and define its parameters. As description, a single phrase will suffice: the spiritual-blues impulse. Cornel West specifies its ground of being: "The black church, black-owned and black-run Christian congregations, is the fountainhead of the Afro-American spiritual-blues impulse."[3] It is the impulse of a defiant people whose existence took shape within a context of monumental oppression; it is the politically charged, cultic back beat of their religious resistance.

And thus West can maintain that "Afro-American music is first and foremost, though not exclusively or universally, a countercultural practice with deep roots in modes of religious transcendence and political opposition."[4] Even where the music is demonstrably, and sometimes even shockingly, secular, the careful observer can trace a developmental path back to black cultic traditions. This Black Church connection is not something unique to black music; it is, according to West, particular to everything about black America. As he puts it, "Without the black church, with its African roots and Christian context, Afro-American culture—in fact, Afro-America itself—is unthinkable."[5]

Nowhere is this connection between black religious tradition and black music more clearly established than in the African American spiritual. Because I have argued elsewhere that the spirituals are the music of slave resistance, I will press the point very briefly here.[6] Three key points require reaffirmation. First, the spiritual is a biblical genre; primary scriptural characters and themes are well represented. The most prevalent of those themes is the exodus liberation. In their music the slaves identified their own horrific existence with that of the Hebrew people bound in Egypt. Not only did they realistically share Israel's plight; they faithfully anticipated a stake in its God-crafted, miraculous liberation. Like Israel in bondage or Jesus on the cross, they saw themselves as God's special people who had endured the injustice of oppression and slaughter through no fault of their own. Like both of them, they would one day be historically redeemed. Until that day came, they sang about the ways they could endure their oppression, escape it, or even—in some unusual cases like those of Nat Turner and Harriet Tubman—fight against it.

Therefore, second, although the spirituals were crafted in a context of desperate, demonic oppression and must always be read against that context if they are to be read correctly, these songs of sorrow were consumed by a message of this-worldly, transformative hope. As James Cone put it, "Trouble is inseparable from the black religious experience. . . . But the spiritual is more than dealing with trouble. It is a joyful experience, a vibrant affirmation of life and its possibilities in an appropriate esthetic form."[7] In other words, and, third, because it sang about the power of God to change life in this world as demonstrably as God had already changed the transcendent world beyond, the spiritual sang a song of historical endurance, hope, and resistance.

So did the blues, albeit in a strikingly secular way. Like the spirituals, the blues are the product of an oppressed African American context. Though the slave circumstance that birthed the spirituals had ended, its aftermath of racial prejudice and injustice endured. Cone speaks to a litany of tragic events like the Hayes Compromise of 1877, which drew federal troops out of the South, thereby leaving black folk at the mercy of Southern racial and political instincts; the 1883 U.S. Supreme Court decision that declared the Civil Rights Act of 1875 unconstitutional; and the 1896 *Plessy v. Ferguson* decision, which upheld the separate but equal foundation of segregation.[8] As he puts it, "by the end of the nineteenth century the political disfranchisement of black people was complete. White people could still do to black people what they willed, just as in slavery days. This was the situation that created the blues."[9]

This continuity of oppression spawned what West saw as a continuous impulse in what turned out to be two very different musical forms. Larry Neal observes that although the worldviews of the spirituals and the blues were quite different, "the music [of the blues] had arisen out of the same feeling which produced the spirituals, jubilees, gospel songs, and work songs."[10] Like the spiritual, the blues sang against the very circumstances of its birth. Cone is specific. He argues, "If the blues are viewed in the proper perspective, it is clear that their mood is very similar to the ethos of the spirituals. Indeed, I contend that the blues and the spirituals flow from the same bedrock of experience, and neither is an adequate interpretation of black life without the commentary of the other."[11] So close are they in impulse that he calls the blues "secular spirituals." Like their "spiritual" counterparts, their focus was resistance. The blues counseled combat against the world, not mere existence within it. "The blues were techniques of survival and expressions of courage. They tell us about the contradictions that black people experienced and what they did to overcome them.

The blues operated from what Anthony Pinn calls the "raw" or "gutbucket" experiences of damaged life lived in a ruinous world so that the world, not the Bible, became the blues singer's primary conversation partner.[12] Teresa Reed observes:

> Unlike the revered and celebrated Negro spiritual of the nineteenth century, the blues spoke in the first person of raw, uncensored, real-life experiences. In its lyrics, subjects like sex, drunkenness, poverty, suicide, violence, and hatred are treated with striking straightforwardness. The defiant, assertive tone of the music is that of a generation of blacks born after slavery and coming of age on the threshold of the twentieth century.[13]

Speaking in intensely personal and individualistic ways, as opposed to the corporate perspective found in the communally oriented spirituals, the blues singer came to believe that transformation would occur only as a result of his own handiwork. Given that he wasn't capable of transforming his entire world, he tried to change as much as he could of his own personal circumstances in very physical, sensual ways. Prevented from making political choices, uninterested in making religious ones, he tried to control his environment by doing what slave males had been unable to do—make sexual choices. As Reed observes, "the issue of sexuality is certainly the most conspicuous and pervasive theme in blues lyrics. . . . For many blacks, romance functioned in much the same way as religion, meeting emotional needs in an immediate and tangible way. And in some cases, the blues text presents romantic intimacy as the preferred alternative to religion."[14] The lyrics of the song "Broke Down Engine" are a case in point:

> Feel like a broke down engine; mama ain't got no driving-wheel
> You ever been down and lonesome; you know just how Willie McTell feels
> I been shooting craps and gambling; good gal and I done got broke

I done pawned my thirty-two special; good gal and my clothes
in soak
I even went to my praying ground; dropped down on bended
knees
I ain't crying for no religion; Lordy give me back my good gal
please.[15]

It is this "earthiness" that earned the blues the epithet "the devil's music."

Equally troublesome to many traditional, churchgoing black Christians was the blues' loss of what Cone calls "objective transcendence": "The blues people, however, sing as if God is irrelevant, and their task is to deal with trouble without special reference to Jesus Christ. This is not atheism; rather it is believing that *transcendence* will only be meaningful when it is made real in and through the limits of historical experience."[16] The focus, and the hope, reside in the black experience that finds a way to overcome the hostility imposed upon it. "Overcoming" is the key. While the blues may not rely upon God as the spirituals do, like the spirituals they resist the oppressive circumstances that have befallen God's black children. They are still "basically defiant in their attitude toward life." It is just that "they are about survival on the meanest, most gut level of human existence."[17]

Secular cadence and symbolism didn't provide the only musical option for post–Civil War, postemancipation black folk in the United States. Also springing forth from the spiritual-blues impulse was gospel. Anthony Pinn describes its genesis this way:

But many of those who sang the blues were also religious in a traditional, church-derived way. Twentieth-century born-again blues folks, most notably Thomas Andrew Dorsey, were responsible for the development of a blues-influenced form of religious music called gospel blues or gospel music that got underway in 1921 with Dorsey's first song, "Someday, Somewhere."[18]

Reed is just as clear about the connection:

Nonetheless, Dorsey himself considered the connection between gospel and blues to be self-evident, as the two styles had a similar emotional effect upon its participants. To him, both were equally valid vehicles of feeling, and the nature of the feeling—sacred or secular—was unimportant. . . . Dorsey's gospel blues demonstrate the African tendency to blend dimensions by reconciling the secular to the sacred.[19]

The link between gospel music and the spirituals was just as strong. Though the contexts of the spiritual—the Southern slave plantation—and gospel music—the urban cities of the great northern black migration at the early part of the twentieth century—were radically different, the situation of oppression to which the different musical forms spoke remained eerily constant. There is no doubt that this shared context of suffering helped forge thematic bonds between the two genres. Both pressed the case that *all* humans were created in God's image, that black people were related to Christ as brother and friend, and that God saw the pain and suffering of black folk and would bring them through it. Like the creators of the spirituals, gospel singers identified closely with the people of Israel and their exodus into liberation as God's chosen people. It was this sense of chosenness, Pinn argues, that allowed gospel singers to counter "manifest destiny arguments by which colonists and their descendants claimed they had been set apart to establish the kingdom of God on earth."[20]

Just as striking is the shared breakdown of temporal boundaries. In both genres, past, present, and future merge in such a way that hope based in the past and promise foreseen in the future became potent present realities. Thus Pinn notes, "Current biblical scholars might be surprised by the freedom with which black religious music brings historical and biblical figures into conversation with their current plight. It would not be uncommon to have Moses present, or Jesus present, as if the community of the enslaved is in direct communication with these figures."[21] When the slave sang, "Were you there when they crucified my Lord?" she asked the question sincerely. As the spiritual and/or gospel singers *were*, through their present struggles, there with Jesus in his past torment, so *are* they with him when he rises to his glory on the third day, *and* when he consolidates his power on the last day.

In the twentieth century, gospel, like its spiritual and blues forebears, helped empower a perspective of resistance. C. Eric Lincoln and Lawrence Mamiya point to the way civil rights leaders joined the forces of gospel and spiritual to create a hybrid musical style, highlighting the civil rights anthem "We Shall Overcome" as "a synthesis of the spiritual 'I'll Be Alright' and the C. A. Tindley [gospel] hymn 'I'll Overcome Someday.' The melody is that of the spiritual, and the lyric a variation on Tindley's text."[22] In Montgomery, Selma, and many other Southern cities, marchers moved to the words, "We shall overcome, we shall overcome, we shall overcome someday. If in our hearts we do believe, we shall overcome someday." Decades earlier, perhaps with a more individual, redemptive objective in mind, the gospel singer had declared, "I'll overcome some day; I'll overcome someday; I'll overcome someday. If in my heart I do not yield, I'll overcome someday."[23] The foundational impulse of resistance was no doubt sufficiently potent and ingrained that harmonizing the genres in an effort to break down oppressive social and political boundaries was an instinctively effective move.

In the current African American musical tradition, there is perhaps no more stunning and creative development than rap music. Indeed, West calls it "the most important development in Afro-American popular music since 1979."[24] Though clearly a popular genre, its home is nonetheless in the very same spiritual-blues impulse. Pinn puts it this way: "The link between earlier forms of musical expression, necessitated by common existential hardships and cultural tools is, once again, forged; this time, the continuity is between blues and rap."[25] Michael Eric Dyson clarifies the connection:

> The blues functioned for another generation of blacks similarly to the way rap functions for young blacks today: as a source of racial identity, permitting forms of boasting and machismo for devalued black men suffering from social emasculation, allowing commentary on social and personal

conditions in uncensored language, and fostering the ability to transform hurt and anguish into art and commerce.[26]

Observers of the phenomenon argue that rap, a powerful combination of black rhetoric and black music, has always had this orientation of political and cultural resistance. Most chart the public debut of the form with songwriter Sylvia Robinson's 1979 recording and release of "Rapper's Delight" by Harlem's Sugarhill Gang.[27] Potent albums like *Raising Hell* from the group Run-DMC followed up with music like the anthem "Proud to Be Black," which Dyson calls "a poignant and provocative hybrid of fiery lyricism and potent critique."[28] Formed from the perspective of young black, mostly males in the urban ghettos of New York and later other large cities, the music lashed out at the oppressive economic, social, and political circumstances that haunted the black lower class and underclass. Aiming to educate and shame not just white society, but also middle- and upper-class black society in a manner similar to the way blues singers lashed out at their more well-to-do churchgoing counterparts, rap artists paint an aesthetic portrait of their world that is as disgustingly shocking as the horrific reality it depicts. West calls it "the musical expression of the paradoxical cry of desperation and celebration of the black underclass and poor working class, a cry which openly acknowledges and confronts the wave of personal cold-heartedness, criminal cruelty, and existential hopelessness in the black ghettos of Afro-America."[29]

Rap expresses its painful view of the world through traditional and historical images that are particularly meaningful for the audience it hopes to energize and that it intends to critique. Even early on, rappers depended on musical traditions of the past for their present riffs. Some called them derivative, others parasitic. Dyson explains that "this first stage in rap record production was characterized by rappers placing their rhythmic repetitive speech and staccatoed syllabic dexterity over well-known black music hits (mostly R&B)."[30] As the genre progressed, so did the sophistication of this technique that would eventually be termed sampling. Pulling images and themes from black music, history, speech, and even religious tradition, the rap artist blended historical moment into contemporary challenge in a way guaranteed to stir passion, demand attention, and even counsel resistance. Pinn is clear:

> Rap lyrics present a postmodern articulation of themes, lifestyles, and behaviors found in Black oral tradition: for example, heroes such as 'Bad Nigger,' Brer Rabbit, Signifying Monkey, Stagolee, and Dolemite. Using these figures and their adventures as a model, rap music develops ways of circumventing powerlessness, outsmarting and temporarily gaining the upper hand over the dominant society.[31]

Speaking more particularly, Dyson observes that the group Public Enemy "is a forceful, prophetic voice in young black culture that holds up historical standards of racial achievement as incentive to combat contemporary forms of racist and classist oppression."[32] Their rap "Party for Your Right to Fight" is an illustrative case in point:

> Power equality, and we're out to get it
> I know some of you ain't wit' it
> This party started right in sixty-six
> With a pro-black radical mix.[33]

Run-DMC's "Proud to Be Black" is another:

> Ya know I'm proud to be black ya'll
> And that's a fact ya'll
> Now Harriet Tubman was born a slave
> She was a tiny black woman when she was raised
> She was livin' to be givin', there's a lot that she gave
> There's not a slave in this day and age
> I'm proud to be black.[34]

The problems—and they are many, according to rap's numerous critics—begin with the genre's apparent refusal to balance an attentiveness to the gritty portrayal of the decimation of life in the inner city with a sense of transcendent, transformative hope. The result is a music form that elicits a feeling of ultimate hopelessness where the only way out is a path of social self-destruction. On the one hand, "status rap" champions a kind of greedy consumerism that glorifies a lifestyle of wealth and excess. Most of its constituents could hope to achieve it only via a life of petty street or institutionalized drug crime. On the other hand, "gangsta rap" worships and thereby elicits the very violence, hatred, and destruction of black lives that rap was ostensibly crafted to decry.[35] At its worst, much of rap music, like its blues brother, tends to degrade women with a misogynistic worldview that not only belittles the female person but views sexual interaction as a social encounter where the stronger dominates the weaker. In such cases, rap champions a cynicism that has no real hope for transformative change. Having seen the worst of society, it too often either lashes out vindictively against it, self-destructively mimics it, or appropriately laments it without ever envisioning the kind of transcendent intervention that could make real change possible. West notes the sad paradox: "Black rap music is surely grounded in the Afro-American spiritual-blues impulse, but certain versions of this music radically call into question the roots of this impulse, the roots of transcendence and opposition. Without a utopian dimension—with transcendence from or opposition to evil—there can be no struggle, no hope, no meaning."[36]

And yet, whether this "utopian" dimension of the spiritual-blues impulse is lived out or is not—as is apparently the case often with blues and rap—resistance remains. Even a study as elementary as this one demonstrates the existence of two primary constants: a context of oppression and an impulse of resistance against it. No matter how much the forms of the impulse change, these two dynamics remain the same. They locate the musical traditions, link them together, and give them their force of life. Just as they do in the case of the nine hymns in the book of Revelation.

The Subject: The Hymns of the Apocalypse

Like rap, Revelation is a dangerous blend of memorable music and recalcitrant rhetoric. But, like the spirituals, Revelation never gives up hope. Its liturgical hymns witness to the promise that God is relieving Rome of its historical command. Right now.

Of the nine hymnic units in the Apocalypse, seven of them (4:8–11; 5:9–14; 7:9–12; 11:5–8; 16:4–6; 19:1–4; 19:5–8) are antiphonal in form: call and response. Hymnic exchanges between angels, cherubim, dead humans, and even the inanimate heavenly altar cascade down to earth and rise back up to the heavens in worshipful celebration of God's identity and God's purpose for human- and heaven-kind. It all begins in 4:8–11, a celebratory declaration of God's transcendent and historical lordship that sets the tone for the hymns that follow. Paced by their threefold testimonial to God's holiness, the four cherubim who guard the throne sing to the majestic status of the Almighty One who is, who unlike human kings, has always been, and who will soon be coming with great and transformative power.[37] It is no accident that they use the same descriptors (Almighty, the One who was, is, and will be) used to communicate either Caesar's or a Greco-Roman god's magnificence.[38] It is no accident that these same two oppositional descriptors are found several times in close relationship with each other, and on almost all of those occasions as integral parts of these hardheaded hymns.[39] It is no accident when the cherubim start, no accident when the twenty-four elders finish by casting down their crowns before God's throne and declaring God not only ruler but creator of all. Human kings showed their deference to Caesar by calling him Lord and God and placing their crowns before him; by their parallel behavior in the heavenly throne room the elders show that such homage belongs solely to God.[40] They sing it clearly so it can be heard forcefully, "You, Lord, God, are worthy." What they mean is, *only* you!

The point that 4:8–11 made for God, 5:9–14 establishes for God's messianic regent, the Lamb. Maintaining the same themes, in many cases with the same language, but in a reverse order of presentation, this hymn sings of the Lamb's worthiness.[41] If, as most critics agree, the seven-sealed scroll holds the details about the plan and purpose of human history, then the one charged to open and read it is the one given charge of that history. It is no accident that the Lamb, and not any human ruler, is the one being, the *only* being worthy of such responsibility. Caesar does not set the course of human life and give it meaning; the Lamb does, by his blood.

As Schüssler Fiorenza notes, "According to Roman law, those prisoners of war who were ransomed were brought back home and reintegrated into their own nation. In the same way, those who were ransomed by Christ for God were liberated in order to constitute here and now a 'kingdom of priests.'"[42] Where Rome is concerned, any such kingdom is unauthorized. Any such unauthorized kingdom is by definition a counterkingdom and therefore a provocation to be challenged. By singing this song, the twenty-four elders dare Rome to bring the challenge on. Backing them up are the voices of myriads of heavenly hosts, who reaffirm the singular worthiness of the Lamb and thereby initiate the bowing down of every creature in heaven, on the earth, and even under the earth (thereby comprising all three tiers of the three-tiered mythological universe) before the Lamb rather than before Caesar. Is that the right move? According to the four cherubim, it is. After opening the initial hymn with their deafening "Holy, holy, holy," they salute the combative claims made in this one with a resounding "Amen!"

Even where the hymnic language seems to be the benign stuff of spiritual salvation and praise, the theme of opposing the Roman regime is palpably present. In 7:9–12, an uncountable soul force composed of those from every tongue, tribe, and nation stands before the heavenly throne and the Lamb, clad in white robes, armed with fronds of palm, and cries out, "Salvation belongs to our God on the throne and to the Lamb."

There are potent political problems with this allegedly otherworldly vision. First, according to Roman imperial rhetoric, every tongue, tribe, and nation owes its peace and salvation exclusively to Caesar. Second, salvation is imaged as a transformative, historical victory. Over whom? For John, there is only Rome. The white robes have already been established as a symbol of victorious conquest over the beastly machinations of imperial Rome (3:4; 4:4; 6:9–11; see also 7:13). The palm fronds represent victory in a broader historical sense.[43] As David Aune points out, "The frequency with which palm fronds occur on Jewish coins together with the name of the current ruler suggests that they symbolize, like the wreath, an ascendant ruler"[44] If Rome *is* the ruler, how can this "salvific" language about an *ascendant* ruler be heard as anything other than political taunting? A new human victory/rule, this apparent kingdom of priests, backed up by this cheering, heavenly throng, is apparently on the rise. Even the heavens believe it. When the angels, twenty-four elders, and four cherubim hear this heavenly call to rhetorical arms, they fall on their faces before God and worship with another resounding Amen.

The fourth antiphonal hymn, 11:15–18, clarifies what the third one left implicit. Not only do boisterous heavenly voices declare victory; they thank God for making it so. As Eugene Boring notes, "usurpers had falsely operated in this world as though they were its rightful lords."[45] Now their time of pretense has come to an end. The kingdom of the world—it has to be Rome—becomes the kingdom of God and the Lamb instead. They, not Caesar, will reign forever. Once again the twenty-four elders respond. They fall before God, the one true Almighty, who, unlike every historical king, both was and now is. No need any longer to add the proclamation that the Almighty is coming; as the trumpet fanfare attests, by this hymnic moment God is already here.

It is all about justice now. In the fifth antiphonal hymnic unit, 16:5–7, the angel of the waters sings accompaniment to the Almighty's destruction of Rome and its political and economic minions. It is the righteous effort of a Holy and just God. The One who is again identified as having championed both past and present history gives back to the evil ones the very wickedness they bestowed on others. The bloodthirsty are made to choke on the very blood they shed. Elated, the altar that had once served as shelter for the souls of those slaughtered for their historical witness to the lordship of Christ responds in hymnic affirmation.[46] God's devastating blow is so fiercely appropriate that even the furniture is compelled to sing.

So, apparently, is everyone else. The sixth hymnic unit (19:1–4) and the seventh (19:5–8) erupt in a hallelujah chorus of affirmation. How thankful are John's choral witnesses to God's judgment?

This is the only place in the New Testament where "Hallelujah, praise Yahweh" occurs.[47] The Almighty God, not Rome, is the ultimate historical judge. As Boring observes, "God has reversed Rome's judgments against the Christians in a higher court."[48] The Almighty God, not Rome, reigns supreme. The hallelujahs rain down in the first hymnic unit as the heavenly multitude twice praises God's salvation as a historical/political liberation that follows immediately from the utter decimation of bloodthirsty, oppressive, and imperial Roman power. The twenty-four elders and four cherubim respond with a corroborating Amen and Hallelujah of their own. This is the very essence of *political* worship. As Boring explains, "Even with all the judgment, the scene never ceases to be a worship scene. The smoke of Babylon that ascends 'forever' is only a grisly contrast to the incense of the heavenly worship (5:8; 8:3–4). Worship celebrates the 'mighty acts of God,' not our pious feelings."[49]

It also celebrates the relationship that now may freely develop between the Lamb and his church. Heretofore, the threat of Roman lordship had stood in the way. John feared that his followers would align themselves with Rome's imperious claims and accommodate themselves to Rome's political and economic prowess in the same way that a weak person might be lured into the sin of prostitution. But now that Rome and its claim to lordship have been justifiably removed, God's people have the freedom to witness properly—which is to say, defiantly. The reward for that witness is symbolized by the imagery of fine linen, bright and pure. Isaiah, as G. K. Beale points out, had already laid the foundational premise: "Isaiah says that there will be rejoicing by those whom God will clothe at the time of Israel's end-time restoration. The clothing represents 'salvation' and 'righteousness,' that is deliverance from captivity."[50] The clothing is an acknowledgment of righteousness. That, Isaiah knew long ago, is why the heavenly multitude sings. "The phrases in Isaiah about the bridegroom and bride . . . emphasize further what the reception of the coming salvation and righteousness from God will be like: it will be like a new, intimate marriage relationship in which bride and bridegroom celebrate by wearing festive apparel."[51]

The other two hymnic units, 12:10–12 and 15:3–4, celebrate the same primary themes; while resisting the lordship of Rome, they proclaim the lordship of God and the Lamb. Nowhere is this slap in the Roman imperial face more evident than at the Lamb's victory hymn of 15:3b–4. A shameless appeal to the song of victory sung following the exodus from Pharaoh, it champions the great and marvelous present deeds of the Almighty as a recapitulation of the legendary, earlier act of God.[52] The difference, as Boring points out, is that while Israel's song focused on the decimation of Pharaoh's army, the song of those who conquer the beast fixates on the awesome power of God.[53] This God, not Rome, is the one Universal Sovereign. All nations knew it long ago. All nations will know it now.

They will know it not only because of God's actions, but because of the conquering behavior, the resistant witness of the Lamb's followers. A heavenly voice sings to their efforts at 12:10–12. They join in God's conquest of Rome by assisting God's effort in demolishing the demonic foundation upon which Rome was built. By the power of the Lamb's blood and their own testimony, they not only witness to the contrary lordship of the Lamb; their very witness has the power to bring that lordship about.

The hymns, then, are a celebration of confrontational resistance. John's hearers and readers live in an oppressive climate, where they will be punished for standing up and standing out against the lordship of Rome. Nevertheless, these hymns incite them to respond to the eschatological worship call of angels, cherubim, elders, and a heavenly multitude of souls with their own politically charged worship and witness to the Almighty status of God and the Lamb.

The Focus: What Do You See?

I see parallels. What are the correspondences between the hymns in Revelation and the music of the spiritual-blues impulse that help us reread Revelation's hymns and surrounding narrative? I can speak briefly to a few. Like the hymns of Revelation, the music of the spiritual-blues impulse is antiphonal. In fact, the spiritual, many historians observe, is itself largely an antiphonal entity. Lincoln and Mamiya explain how many spirituals developed as the slave pastor preached and the congregation called back with a rhythmic reply. "Little by little this musical call and response became a song."[54] The interplay between singer and congregation/audience is an indelible component in the music that continues from this original "spiritual" impulse. The resistance theme of the music is applauded, affirmed, and anticipated as a way of actual living when the respondent answers the initial hymnic call with a vocalization of his own. The respondent who cries out, "Sing it!" might just as well be commanding her vocalist and fellow parishioners to "Live it!" It is no wonder that Cone calls this "functional" music. He writes: "Black music, then, is not an artistic creation for its own sake; rather it tells us about the *feeling* and *thinking* of African people, and the kinds of mental adjustments they had to make in order to survive in an alien land."[55]

Perhaps John presents most of his hymns as antiphonal constructions precisely because he wants to tap into the kind of functionality that is characteristic of the call-and-response heritage of music in the spiritual-blues impulse. Perhaps, as one heavenly agent declares God's lordship and Almighty status and another responds with the resounding "Sing it!" of the amens, hallelujahs, and the like, John hopes his all-too-human hearers and readers will be challenged to raise a living, antiphonal response of their own. What Schüssler Fiorenza concludes about the larger narrative of the Apocalypse can in this way now also be seen as a primary directive for the hymns. "Revelation provides the vision of an alternative world in order to motivate the audience to strengthen their resistance in the face of Babylon/Rome's overwhelming threat to destroy their life and livelihood."[56] *Their* response to the hymnic praise of the Lamb's lordship should be a going forth defiantly to bring that rhythmic resistance to life.

If the call and response *form* proves by itself to be an insufficient prodding of resistant behavior, then perhaps a strategic sampling of victorious moments from the people's past will add the necessary, complementary *content*. In every form of the spiritual-blues impulse that I have considered, this appeal to key historical

African American moments has played this kind of provocative role.[57] Sometimes these moments are mentioned as straightforward examples of successful past African American resistance. Other times they are merged with key moments in the historical life of the people Israel or the Jesus of the canonical Gospels. In this latter way, African American history merges with biblical history so that it becomes clear that in spite of, and perhaps because of, their oppression, this people has a uniquely powerful relationship with God. As God once redeemed and vindicated Israel and Jesus, so God will redeem and vindicate them.

The most intriguing case is again that of rap. When "sampling," the rap artist recalls the past in a way that encourages resistance in the present. In doing so, however, rap is not originating something new but building upon a musical legacy well established in the spiritual-blues impulse out of which it grew. As Dyson puts it, rap's "messages of historical remembrance and prophetic social criticism connect it to a powerful history of African-American cultural resistance, rebellion, and revolution. The values of memory and social criticism link us with a racial past to which we can resolutely and hopefully appeal in resisting present forms of social hopelessness, historical amnesia, and cultural nihilism."[58]

The hymns in Revelation appear to pursue the same goal of resistance with the same strategy of remembrance. The 15:3–4 hymn, which explicitly calls to mind the song of Moses following the crossing of the Red Sea, is only the tip of the antiphonal iceberg. The singers and responders in all the hymns use language that, recalling for John's hearers and readers victorious moments from Israel's past, assures that God's protection and promise will be with those who stand with God and stand for God's lordship in the present. No wonder Aune can conclude: "It now appears that John did not quote or modify traditional Jewish or Christian hymns with which he was familiar; rather he wrote new hymns for their present context making use of some traditional Jewish and Christian liturgical traditions and forms, including the hallelujah, the Amen, the *sanctus* (4:8), doxologies (5:13; 7:10, 12; 19:1) and acclamations (4:11; 5:9,12)."[59] For what reason? Apparently, as with the musicians of the spiritual-blues impulse, John recalls the past in order to charge people up in the present.

This is easier to accomplish when the boundaries that separate past, present, and future are breached by the music. Those who respond to the music are therefore able to sense the presence of God with God's people in past moments of victory like the exodus and the resurrection, and sense the realization of God's future promise, all without leaving the present moment. Music can do that. Highlighting the spirituals, Reed writes about a rendition of "Open the Window, Noah" ("Norah, Hist the Windah"): "By speaking directly to Noah as though he were present, the poet removes the Bible character from the mystical past and places him in the 'here and now.'"[60] Why? So that Noah's victory can become the slave's victory. This is precisely why in John's liturgical hymns not only the boundaries between heaven and earth are broken down, but the ones that separate time as well. The 15:3–4 song about Moses' past victory, which is simultaneously a pointer to God's future victory, is a dramatic case in point; it has a real-time, present effect. Reddish makes an appropriate observation: "While in John's vision it is an eschatological song, in the real world of John's day this was a song that was already being sung. The victory that was in the future was being anticipated in the present."[61]

Though this music was intended to shore up the church, John must have known—apparently did intend—that it would also threaten Rome. Though its symbolic use of biblical imagery is imitated in the language of the spirituals, the musical kinship in this case is much closer to rap. Rap language is often "in your face" language. It hijacks the language and imagery of contemporary, everyday Euro-American life, subverts it, and then gives it a rebellious twist. Rap uses the language of American culture to threaten the hold American culture has over African Americans, particularly young, urban, underclass African Americans. Though most rap wasn't written for white America, rap very much directs its message to white America. It wants to be overheard preaching a message of resistance, even as it intends this message for its own black constituents. The more I read Revelation through this lens, the more I am convinced that John, too, targeted his adversary Rome, as one of his primary audiences. John wants the Romans to recognize themselves in his hymnic imagery, but his purpose is not flattery but critique. As Aune notes, John knows that "the Romans (borrowing from the Hellenistic kingship traditions) developed an elaborate imperial court ceremonial that included the singing of hymns and the shouting of acclamations to the emperor by those present in court (Dio Cassius 59.24.5; Tacitus *Annals* 14:15; Suetonius *Nero* 20.3)."[62] John uses this "similarity between the hymns in Revelation and the imperial hymns composed in honor of the emperor" to demonstrate that the qualities claimed for the emperor actually belonged solely to God.[63] Schüssler Fiorenza is even more specific:

> The Roman Emperor Augustus, for instance, was called 'savior of the Greeks and of the whole inhabited world,' 'savior and benefactor,' 'savior and founder,' and 'savior and god.' His birthday marked the beginning of 'good tidings' (gospels). He was regarded as the 'just and generous lord' whose reign sustained peace and happiness, that is, salvation. By utilizing these terms, the heavenly choir asserts: It is not the power of Caesar but God's power and salvation that is revealed in the justice meted out to Babylon/Rome and to its vassals and provinces.[64]

John took their language, subverted it, and used it for his own resistant, oppositional cause. In this light, all the earlier scholarly talk that John was symbolically coded so that the Romans wouldn't feel threatened by the claims of his narrative feels catastrophically off base. John wasn't hiding his claims from Rome; he was directing them to Rome. He wanted Rome to hear his songs and know that his people were singing in antiphonal response to them. He wanted Rome to know that God's future lordship was taking place in the present, that God's people had committed themselves to standing up for that lordship, and that God was even now standing with them and against Rome. John the hymnist was John the rapper. He was not hiding from a fight; he was picking one.

And he was picking it with the certainty that the transcendent God was going to fight on his side. It is this absolute certainty of

God's interventionist presence and power that some observers might say is a point of separation between the hymns in Revelation and some of the key music of spiritual-blues impulse. Spirituals and gospel music clearly rely on a sense of God's transcendent presence, but many critics have argued that blues and rap do not have such a transcendent sense. In fact, the earthiness of the blues directly contradicts John's assurance that God is a part of every element of human living, even something as seemingly benign (to many of the Christians in John's churches!) as eating meat left over from a service commemorating pagan idols.

It is not with the blues, however, that I find the most fascinating point of contradictory contact. I find that with rap. Most of the theologically oriented observers of rap music highlight what they call its disturbing lack of theological transcendence. And yet, in considering the rap music of Tupac Shakur, a representative of gangsta rap, through the eyes of Teresa Reed, author of *The Holy Profane: Religion in Black Popular Music*, I find even here, in the midst of the horrific circumstances that surrounded his own life and those of his colleagues and kin, a belief not only in God, but that God held the transformative key for human life. In making her case for a sense of the transcendent in Shakur's rap music, Reed appeals first to his hymn "God Bless the Dead," a homage to peers who died before him. What strikes her, she says, "is that despite the troubling nature of Tupac's lifestyle, he emerges in these lyrics as a man of faith—a man who clearly believes in God, prays to God, and envisions an afterlife. His peers fall victim to an irrational and violent world, yet Tupac's emotional proximity to God is such that he asks, 'why did You have to take a good one?'"[65] The souls slaughtered in heaven in Revelation 6:9–11 challenge God with a similar question: how long before you intervene? The hymns answer with a declaration that the intervention is already underway. According to Reed's reading of Shakur's language, he too believed that God had already intervened through Jesus' life and death. Shakur saw, as John saw, that Jesus' death was the key to understanding human death and to the victorious opposition to it. She quotes from his song "Hail Mary": "And God said He should send His one begotten Son to lead the wild into the ways of the man. . . . Follow me. . . . Eat my flesh, flesh of my flesh." Her assessment:

> Tupac's subtle, yet clever connection of Christ's death to his own extends a poetic tradition that was born during the antebellum era. Black slaves always likened their suffering to that of Biblical figures, as numerous Negro spirituals illustrate. . . . I would say the same about Tupac and "Hail Mary." References to Christ in this rap are salient because the rapper connects Christ's suffering to his own.[66]

In another song, "Unconditional Love," he raps, "How many caskets can we witness/Before we see it's hard to live life without God/so we must ask forgiveness." She understands him to mean: "Violence and death are the result of living life apart from God." She goes on to conclude: "Tupac's religious self-assessment included both an acknowledgement of his distance from God coupled with a strong belief in God's redemptive power."[67]

Finally, in a song called "Black Jesuz" Tupac declared Black Jesus as the messiah who had and could share the kind of strength necessary to survive life in the ghetto, who suffered and hurt as young urban blacks do, and yet who overcame and as a result gave the promise of overcoming to them. Looking at similar portraits sprinkled through the otherwise brutal, harsh, violent, misogynist, and destructive language of Shakur's gangsta rap, Reed can still draw this rather astounding conclusion: "Most important, perhaps, Tupac's legacy shows how the gangster, the thug, the outlaw, can fill our ears with bad words and ugly, brutal truths, all the while pointing us to pictures of a caring God."[68]

That, after all, is in many ways also the perfect conclusion to draw about the book of Revelation and the hymns that bring it to liturgical life. They are fierce, apparently unflinching looks at life lived under Roman occupation and oppression. And yet they picture a God who cares. And they sing out for that God to intervene in ways that are appropriate to the hostile circumstance in which God will find his struggling folk.

We can no longer place the eschatological hymns of the Apocalypse in the exact contextual framework in which John first heard and relayed them. We therefore lose much of their original resistant intent in their exegetical translation to our own time and place. That is why it is helpful to look at them in the light of contemporary music that we can more confidently place in context. Perhaps as we study the resistant music of our own time, music that rails against the evils of the Romes of our own time, we may better understand and appreciate the hymns John heard the angels, cherubim, elders, souls, and altar singing in his time.

We see almost immediately how mistrusted such music tends to be. Because of the challenges it raises, this music conjures the fear that it will bring down upon its singers and those related to them the very evils it showcases and confronts. The spirituals and gospel music are, in this case, less problematic than the blues and rap. Because of their religious encoding and biblical imagery, the former, though still the music of resistance, found a warmer African American and even Euro-American reception. Blues and rap, though, in this regard, correspond to the canonical place of Revelation; though they were a part of the spiritual-blues impulse—just as Revelation was a part of the epistolary impulse of first-century Christianity—their radical approach sets them negatively apart. Two shared attributes stand out: the violence and the misogyny. There is no doubt that, like Revelation, blues and rap entertain a damaging view of women that, while degrading them as sexual objects, tends also to see them as the ultimate cause of destructive human behavior in the world. And no one who reads Revelation seriously can escape shuddering at the cosmic-scale destruction that takes place as heaven meets satanic lethal force with an angelic lethal force of its own. Violence described and violence enjoined are classic hallmarks of many expressions of rap.

How can this descriptive similarity between Revelation's hymns, blues, and particularly rap help us in our reading and, perhaps, our appreciation of what John is doing in Revelation? It helps us first by continually reminding us as readers that just as blues and rap are an integral part of the spiritual-blues impulse and could not have arisen without that foundation—and must therefore harbor much of their musical DNA within their radically different forms—so Revelation, as much as even Christians deride it, remains an integral part of the Christian impulse to save and not destroy. Its imagery ultimately seeks the redemption and not the destruction of humankind. And for that reason it is perhaps well to remember that Revelation champions an innumerable heavenly multitude from all nations and tongues (7:9). It is not people that Revelation sings against; it is Rome and those who, enslaved by its political and economic domination, seek to consolidate their power and use it against those who will not bow down before it.

When reading Revelation, we should never read it outside of its context as a vital part of the Christian impulse. Its violence and even its misogyny should be read in light of that overall impulse, and thus seen to be the vicious aberrations that they are—aberrations that mirror the world perspective in which John writes but are ultimately themselves the targets of John's transformative vision, even though he was himself too caught up in that environment to see that.

I am suggesting, therefore, that when we approach the music of the blues and rap we start not with the blues and rap but with the spiritual-blues impulse out of which they come. In that way we can see both how blues and rap live up to that impulse and how they stray from it and therefore make themselves subject to the very calls to transformative resistance of the impulse that gave them birth. Just so with Revelation. In reading it, particularly through the window of its hymns, perhaps we should not start with the violence and misogyny as the primary opening through which we read the text. Perhaps we should start with the salvific impulse that gives Revelation birth, and through that impulse see how Revelation stands up and falls short. But in that case we will not eliminate Revelation's larger, more powerful, transformative message of hope against hopelessly ingrained social and political ill, even when they are found in the text of Revelation itself.

We will also understand better why Revelation appeals to so many nonmainstream Christian groups in a way eerily parallel to the manner in which rap finds acceptance among so many socially, politically, and economically displaced African Americans. As Pinn appropriately puts it, "rappers, without question, must be held responsible for the oppression supported in their music. At the same time, however, critics and fans must recognize that . . . rap echoes oppressive precepts acknowledged and encouraged by the wider society."[69] Both Revelation and rap represent oppressive circumstances that are running rampant in their respective societies, even their respective Christian societies; unless critics take the time actually to take in the view from these societal mirrors before hurling stones at them, they will miss opportunities for changing not only their world but also themselves and their communities. Perhaps in revealing the Christian impulse in its own locally flawed way, Revelation does a service to Christianity that a more acceptable apocalyptic display would have missed. Dyson says it this way:

> Only by confronting the powerful social criticism that rap culture articulates can we hope to understand its appeal to millions of black and white youth. And by examining its weaknesses and blindness, we are encouraged to critically confront our similar shortcomings, which do not often receive the controversial coverage given to rap culture. In so doing, we may discover that many of the values that are openly despised in rap culture [or Revelation, for that matter] are more deeply rooted and widely shared than most of us would care to admit.[70]

For this reason I believe that what Anthony Pinn says about the music of the spiritual-impulse could just as reasonably be said about the hymns and narratives of Revelation:

> As a note of importance, this does not suggest an endorsement of the oppressive opinions held within the blues or other forms of musical expression such as rap. However, I am not willing to reject these musical forms of expression simply because they contain some of the misguided tendencies of the larger society. Rather I am suggesting that the positive

expressions of this music (i.e., the examples of this music which have a constructive intention) suggest a hermeneutic which is worthy of investigation and implementation.[71]

They are, all of them—spirituals, blues, gospel, rap, and the Revelation hymns—fighting music. They are, all of them, in their own way, rapping on Rome. Rome has always been something more than the historical entity that thought to capture the ancient world and chart its course. Rome, even for John, symbolized the human inclination to set oneself up in opposition to the intentions of God, and thereby claim for oneself God's privileged position as the Almighty. For John, historical Rome wasn't new in this regard; it merely followed the mutinous human pattern already established by even more ancient powers like Babylon. Rome too, for all her claims to special status and unique imperial identity, was nothing more than a miserable, demonically driven mimic. So, for people of faith, were all the Romes that would follow the great empire's metaphorical lead. The "Roman" force of American slavery and the institutionalized racism that followed in its wake were mimics of the same idolatrous belief that some humans maintained about their own superior, Almighty status.

It is no wonder that African Americans faced down their imperial power with the same double-edged sword wielded by the Christians of Asia Minor—Music. In oppressive camps where the powers concentrated against you appear limitless in their scope and evil intent, where, defenseless, you stand with neither ally nor hope, where, though you cannot realistically fight back, you refuse to give up and give in, you can still resist. You can sing.

Notes

Chapter 1: The Revelation of Culture

1. Brian K. Blount, *Cultural Interpretation: Reorienting New Testament Criticism* (Minneapolis: Fortress Press, 1995); Brian K. Blount, "If You Get *MY* Meaning: Introducing Cultural Exegesis," in *Exegese und Theoriediskussion*, ed. Stefan Alkier and Ralph Brucker (Tübingen and Basel: Francke-Verlag, 1998), 77–97; Brian K. Blount, *Go Preach! Mark's Kingdom Message and the Black Church Today* (Maryknoll, NY: Orbis Books, 1998); Brian K. Blount, "Reading Revelation Today: Witness as Active Resistance," *Interpretation* 54 (2000): 398–412.

2. M. Eugene Boring, *Revelation* (Louisville, Ky.: John Knox Press, 1989), 54; Elisabeth Schüssler Fiorenza, *The Book of Revelation: Justice and Judgment* (Minneapolis: Fortress Press, 1998), 185.

3. See, for example, the discussion on contemporary historical critical views of the Apocalypse in Arthur Wainwright, *Mysterious Apocalypse: A History of the Interpretation of the Book of Revelation* (Nashville: Abingdon Press, 1993), esp. 125–39.

4. Stephen D. Moore, "Introduction," *Semeia* 82 (1998): viii: "What, then, does cultural studies have to offer biblical studies? What else but a means of *critically* reading the Bible in its present contexts."

5. John Storey, "Introduction: The Study of Popular Culture within Cultural Studies," in *Cultural Theory and Popular Culture: A Reader*, ed. John Storey (London: Harvester & Wheatsheaf, 1994), viii.

6. Stuart Hall, "Cultural Studies and Its Theoretical Legacies," in *Cultural Studies*, ed. Lawrence Grossberg, Cary Nelson, and Paula A. Treichler (New York and London: Routledge Press, 1992), 278.

7. Angela McRobbie, "Post-Marxism and Cultural Studies: A Postscript," in *Cultural Studies*, ed. Lawrence Grossberg, Cary Nelson, and Paula A. Treichler (New York and London: Routledge Press, 1992), 722.
8. Ibid.
9. Cary Nelson, Lawrence Grossberg, and Paula A. Treichler, "Cultural Studies: An Introduction," in *Cultural Studies*, ed. Lawrence Grossberg, Cary Nelson, and Paula A. Treichler (New York and London: Routledge Press, 1992), 2.
10. Ibid., 1.
11. Cited in John Storey, "Cultural Studies: An Introduction," in *What Is Cultural Studies? A Reader*, ed. John Storey (London: Arnold Press, 1996), 1.
12. Nelson, Grossberg, and Treichler, "Cultural Studies: An Introduction," 5.
13. John Storey, *Cultural Studies and the Study of Popular Culture: Theories and Methods* (Athens: University of Georgia Press, 1996), 2.
14. Stuart Hall, "Cultural Studies: Two Paradigms," in *What Is Cultural Studies? A Reader*, ed. John Storey (London: Arnold Press, 1996), 38.
15. Ibid., 36.
16. Storey, *Cultural Studies and the Study of Popular Culture*, 4.
17. See for example McRobbie, "Post-Marxism and Cultural Studies," 723–26; Hall, "Cultural Studies and Its Theoretical Legacies," 280. In cataloguing the problems with Marxism for cultural studies, he lists "its orthodoxy, its doctrinal character, its determinism, its reductionism, its immutable law of history, its status as a metanarrative." While Hall points to the contributions of Gramsci in moving the thinking of cultural studies beyond its early interest in Marxist principles, McRobbie points to the work of Ernesto Laclau as similarly helpful.
18. Storey, "Cultural Studies: An Introduction," 3: "Cultural studies insists that culture's importance derives from the fact that it helps constitute the structure and shape the history."
19. Storey, "Cultural Studies: An Introduction," 3.
20. McRobbie, "Post-Marxism and Cultural Studies," 722.
21. Stephen D. Moore, "Between Birmingham and Jersualem: Cultural Studies and Biblical Studies," *Semeia* 82 (1998): 13.
22. Hall, "Cultural Studies and Its Theoretical Legacies," 281.
23. Storey, "Introduction: The Study of Popular Culture within Cultural Studies," ix.
24. Cf. Storey, "Introduction: The Study of Popular Culture within Cultural Studies," ix: "Hall contends that 'meaning is always a social production, a practice. The world has to be *made to mean*.' Therefore, because different meanings can be ascribed to the same cultural text or practice, meaning is always the site and result of struggle."
25. Nelson, Grossberg, and Treichler, "Cultural Studies: An Introduction," 5.
26. McRobbie, "Post-Marxism and Cultural Studies," 721.

27. Ralph Broadbent, "Ideology, Culture, and British New Testament Studies: The Challenge of Cultural Studies," *Semeia* 82 (1998): 35.
28. Ibid., 36.
29. Ibid., 37.
30. Ibid., 38.
31. Broadbent, "Ideology, Culture, and British New Testament Studies," 38: "English was for Leavis openly ideological. It was not a neutral academic subject. English literature and its study exemplified what it was to be English."
32. See Broadbent, "Ideology, Culture, and British New Testament Studies," 45.
33. See J. Cheryl Exum and Stephen D. Moore, "Biblical Studies/Cultural Studies," in *Biblical Studies/Cultural Studies: The Third Sheffield Colloquium*, ed. J. Cheryl Exum and Stephen D. Moore (Sheffield: Sheffield Academic Press, 1998), 20–21.
34. Moore, "Introduction," vii.
35. Nelson, Grossberg, and Treichler, "Cultural Studies: An Introduction," 12.
36. Moore, "Between Birmingham and Jerusalem," 3.
37. Broadbent, "Ideology, Culture, and British New Testament Studies," 44.
38. Exum and Moore, "Biblical Studies/Cultural Studies," 21.
39. Broadbent, "Ideology, Culture, and British New Testament Studies," 46.
40. Exum and Moore, "Biblical Studies/Cultural Studies," 21; Moore, "Between Birmingham and Jerusalem," 4; ibid.
41. Broadbent, "Ideology, Culture, and British New Testament Studies," 46.
42. See Broadbent, "Ideology, Culture, and British New Testament Studies," 50.
43. Broadbent, "Ideology, Culture, and British New Testament Studies," 51. Cf. Morna Hooker, *The Gospel according to Saint Mark* (Peabody, MA: Hendrickson Publishers, 1991).
44. R. S. Sugirtharajah, "Imperial Critical Commentaries: Christian Discourse and Commentarial Writings in Colonial India," *JSNT* 73 (1999): 93.
45. Ibid., 89.
46. Broadbent, "The Challenge of Cultural Studies," 55–56.
47. Moore, "Between Birmingham and Jerusalem," 7.
48. Exum and Moore, "Biblical Studies/Cultural Studies," 23.
49. Moore, "Between Birmingham and Jerusalem," 9.
50. Hall, "Cultural Studies and Its Theoretical Legacies," 283.
51. Moore, "Between Birmingham and Jerusalem," 12.
52. Cf. Hall, "Cultural Studies and Its Theoretical Legacies," 282–83; Moore, "Between Birmingham and Jerusalem," 12.
53. Paul Gilroy, "Cultural Studies and Ethnic Absolutism," in *Cultural Studies*, ed. Lawrence Grossberg, Cary Nelson, and Paula A. Treichler (New York and London: Routledge Press, 1992), 187.
54. Moore, "Between Birmingham and Jerusalem," 9.
55. Ibid., 10.
56. Ibid.

57. Ibid.
58. Quoted in Moore, "Between Birmingham and Jerusalem," 11.
59. Moore, "Between Birmingham and Jerusalem," 21.
60. Cf. Fernando F. Segovia and Mary Ann Tolbert, eds., *Reading from This Place: Social Location and Biblical Interpretation in Global Perspective.* Volume 2 (Minneapolis: Fortress Press, 1995).
61. Moore, "Between Birmingham and Jerusalem," 21.
62. Fernando F. Segovia, *Decolonizing Biblical Studies: A View from the Margins* (Maryknoll, NY: Orbis Books, 2000), 42.
63. See Segovia, *Decolonizing Biblical Studies*, 3–51, for a fuller discussion.
64. Segovia, *Decolonizing Biblical Studies*, 19.
65. Ibid.
66. Ibid.
67. Ibid., 33.
68. Ibid., 45–46.
69. Exum and Moore, "Biblical Studies/Cultural Studies," 35.
70. R. S. Sugirtharajah, "A Brief Memorandum on Postcolonialism and Biblical Studies," *JSNT* 73 (1999): 5.
71. Tina Pippin, *Death and Desire: The Rhetoric of Gender in the Apocalypse of John* (Louisville, Ky.: Westminster John Knox Press, 1992), 27.
72. Ibid., 16.
73. Ibid., 25.
74. Ibid., 27.
75. Ibid., 16.
76. Ibid., 22.
77. Ibid., 53.
78. Ibid., 80.
79. Pippin, *Death and Desire*, 98–99: "The believers who are called to 'patient endurance' must resist nonviolently, but this resistance is active, not passive, since the result of being a witness (read 'martyr') might be death."
80. Pippin, *Death and Desire*, 80.
81. Catherine Keller, *Apocalypse Now and Then: A Feminist Guide to the End of the World* (Boston: Beacon Press, 1996), 1.
82. Ibid., xiii.
83. Ibid., 11.
84. Ibid., 20.
85. David L. Barr, "Towards an Ethical Reading of the Apocalypse: Reflections on John's Use of Power, Violence, and Misogyny," in *Society of Biblical Literature 1997 Seminar Papers* (Atlanta: Scholars Press, 1997), 360.
86. Ibid., 359–60.
87. Ibid., 361.
88. Ibid.
89. Ibid., 365.

90. Ibid.
91. Ibid.
92. Barr, "Towards an Ethical Reading of the Apocalypse," 365. See also Dorothy A. Lee, "The Heavenly Woman and the Dragon: ReReadings of Revelation 12," in *Feminist Poetics of the Sacred: Creative Suspicions*, ed. Frances Devlin-Glass and Lyn McCredden (Oxford: Oxford University Press, 2001), 198–220. Lee presents a female scholarly reading that is an alternative to Pippin's. She points to the multivalent nature of these ancient stories. This quality allows the stories to be read by women in changing circumstances with very different results. She wants a reading where patriarchy is laid bare and not part of Revelation's reinterpretation. As an example, she focuses on chapter 12 and the woman clothed with the sun. After concluding that the depiction in the chapter is hopelessly patriarchal, she still sees possibilities for rereading the text in a way that is hopeful for women. "Whatever else we may say about the myth, the hero is undeniably female and the intended readers (male and female) are invited to see themselves, collectively and individually, in female guise" (206). She goes on to celebrate the kind of power represented in the woman as opposed to the power symbolized by the dragon. The reader is given two different power options, and the narrative clearly suggests that the woman is the appropriate model. "Combined with the gender identification outlined earlier, the heavenly woman confronts the reader as a striking example of female authority. The wondrous power of the heavenly woman accrues to the sympathetic reader" (208). The woman, then, in her reading, becomes a powerful example of witness resistance, an example that challenges the more sweeping conclusion by Pippin that the text is simply irredeemable for women readers. "In this way, the myth can be read in relation to women's struggle against injustice" (210). See also Elisabeth Schüssler Fiorenza, *The Book of Revelation: Justice and Judgment*, 2nd Edition (Minneapolis: Fortress Press, 1998), 216–19. In a compact discussion of her own perspective on "Reading Gender in Revelation," Schüssler Fiorenza simultaneously critiques the exclusive gender readings of Pippin and Susan Garrett (*Women's Bible Commentary*). Schüssler Fiorenza complains that both scholars miss the complexity of John's symbolism and therefore end up equating his feminine metaphors with real wo/men. She points instead to "the vacillation and ambiguity of a text that slips and slides between feminine and urban characterization, between masculine and beastly symbolization" (217). In her view, this literal equation of the metaphor and real women distorts and disempowers the meaning potential of John's symbolic language. "Overinterpreting the text in gender terms negates the possibility of readers' ethical decision and resistance insofar as it does not leave a rhetorical space for wo/men who desire to read Revelation 'otherwise'" (217).
93. Barr, "Towards an Ethical Reading of the Apocalypse," 367.
94. Allan A. Boesak, *Comfort and Protest: The Apocalypse from a South African Perspective* (Philadelphia: Westminster Press, 1987), 69.

124   *Notes*

95. Ibid., 72.
96. Ibid., 72–73.
97. Miroslav Volf, *Exclusion and Embrace: A Theological Exploration of Identity, Otherness, and Reconciliation* (Nashville: Abingdon Press, 1996), 296.
98. Ibid.
99. Ibid., 279.
100. Ibid., 298.
101. Ibid., 299.
102. Ibid.
103. Ibid., 303.
104. Ibid., 304.

Chapter 2: Can I Get a Witness?

1. Charles Mabee, *Reading Sacred Texts through American Eyes: Biblical Interpretation as Cultural Critique* (Macon, GA: Mercer University Press, 1991), 3.
2. Elisabeth Schüssler Fiorenza, *Revelation: Vision of a Just World* (Minneapolis: Fortress Press, 1991), 64.
3. Adela Yarbro Collins, "The Political Perspective of the Revelation to John," *Journal of Biblical Literature* 96 (1977): 243.
4. Ibid.
5. Ibid., 245.
6. See Brian K. Blount, *Cultural Interpretation: Reorienting New Testament Criticism* (Minneapolis: Fortress Press, 1995) for a fuller discussion of my approach to sociolinguistics for biblical inquiry.
7. Elisabeth Schüssler Fiorenza, *The Book of Revelation: Justice and Judgment* (Minneapolis: Fortress Press, 1998), 193. Fiorenza goes on to enumerate the devotional proclivities of the particular cities where John's churches were located: Ephesus, seat of the proconsul, competed with Pergamum for primacy; Smyrna, a center of the emperor cult; Pergamum, center of the emperor cult, already in 29 BCE had permission to build a temple to the divine Augustus and the goddess Roma; Thyatira, emperor worshipped as Apollo incarnate, son of Zeus; Sardis, in 26 CE competed with other cities for right to build a temple in honor of the emperor, lost out to Smyrna; Laodicea, wealthy city that prospered under the Flavians.
8. C. Eric Lincoln and Lawrence H. Mamiya, *The Black Church in the African American Experience* (Durham and London: Duke University Press, 1990), 1.
9. Anthony B. Pinn, *The Black Church in the Post–Civil Rights Era* (Maryknoll, NY: Orbis Books, 2002), xii.
10. Ibid., xii–xiii.
11. Lincoln and Mamiya, *The Black Church*, 3.
12. Peter J. Paris, *The Social Teaching of the Black Churches* (Philadelphia: Fortress Press, 1985), 7.

13. Anthony B. Pinn, *Terror and Triumph: The Nature of Black Religion* (Minneapolis: Fortress Press, 2003), 88.
14. For a fuller discussion, see Brian K. Blount, *Then the Whisper Put On Flesh: New Testament Ethics in an African American Context* (Nashville: Abingdon Press, 2001).
15. Lincoln and Mamiya, *The Black Church*, 202–3: Gabriel Prosser, 1800: near Richmond; Denmark Vesey, 1822: Charleston, SC; Nat Turner, 1831: Southampton, VA.
16. Pinn, *Terror and Triumph*, 89.
17. Ibid., 90.
18. Pinn, *The Black Church*, 12.
19. Ibid., 13.
20. Pinn, *Terror and Triumph*, 102.
21. Ibid., 103.
22. Ibid., 94.
23. Paris, *Social Teaching*, 11.
24. Andrew Billingsley, *Mighty Like a River: The Black Church and Social Reform* (New York and Oxford: Oxford University Press, 1999), xxii.
25. Lincoln and Mamiya, *The Black Church*, 4.
26. Pinn, *Terror and Triumph*, 94.
27. Billingsley, *Mighty Like a River*, xxii.
28. H. Strathmann, "μάρτυς, μαρτυρέω, μαρτυρία . . . ," *TDNT* 4: 476.
29. Allison A. Trites, "*Martus* and Martyrdom in the Apocalypse: A Semantic Study," *Novum Testamentum* 15 (1973): 72. Trites tracks the transformation over the course of five separate stages. In the first, *martys* simply meant a witness in a court of law, without any expectation of death. In the second phase, which he connects most closely to the time in which John was writing, the word group had come to indicate someone who testified to his faith in a law court and died because of it. In other words, here was a kind of prophetic figure who went into court knowing that the words he would say might cost him his life. Resisting the temptation to save his life by remaining silent or conveying other words that would have been more tolerably accepted, he said them anyway. In the third phase, which Trites feels does evidence itself in its very earliest stages in John's time and writing, death is inextricably tied to witness. Still, even at this point, death is not the primary component. That occurs only at the fourth stage, where a person's death is highlighted; then in the fifth stage the idea of witnessing disappears altogether, and a "martyr" becomes someone who dies for his or her faith. These latter two stages of meaning don't occur until well into the second century, well after John had finished his work. (See Trites, 72–75.)
30. Fred Mazzaferri, "MARTYRIA IĒSOU Revisited," *Bible Translator* 39 (1988): 116.

31. Revelation 1:2 and 1:9 even speak to the testimony or "witness" of Jesus. Loren Johns points out that before John identifies Jesus as the Lamb, he uses some *thirty* other terms to describe Christ. See Loren Johns, *The Lamb Christology of the Apocalypse of John* (Tübingen: Mohr-Siebeck, 2003), 162.

32. Trites, *"Martus* and Martyrdom," 76.

33. See M. Eugene Boring, *Revelation* (Louisville, Ky.: John Knox Press, 1989), 82; David Aune, *Revelation 1–5*, vol 52a of Word Biblical Commentary (Dallas: Word Books, 1997), clxxvii–clxxviii.

34. For a fuller treatment of the grammatical discussion and relevant sources, see Brian K. Blount, "Reading Revelation Today: Witness as Active Resistance," *Interpretation* 54 (2000): 401–2.

35. Careful readers will also recognize an epexegetical *kai* between "firstborn of the dead" and "ruler of the kings of the earth." As was the case with the *kai* that separated "word of God" and "testimony of Jesus," the correlative here indicates that the second term is actually an aspect of the first. It should grammatically read "firstborn of the dead, who is the ruler of the kings of the earth."

36. Cf. Blount, "Reading Revelation Today," 405–6.

37. See Mitchell G. Reddish, *Revelation* (Macon, GA: Smyth & Helwys, 2001), 130; Boring, *Revelation*, 125.

38. Anthony B. Pinn, *Why, Lord? Suffering and Evil in Black Theology* (New York: Continuum, 1995), 39: "Most notably, planters feared the blurring of the line between economic productivity and the slave's humanity. And so, every avenue by which such ideas could enter the mind of Southern slaves had to be closed. This of necessity included the humanizing potential of the gospel. Therefore, in order to avoid contact between slaves and these dangerous ideas, religious instruction and activity for slaves were held to a minimum."

39. Pinn, *Terror and Triumph*, 81.

40. Ibid., 217.

41. Cf. Reddish, *Revelation*, 130–31, where he cites Pss. 6:3; 13:1–2; 35:17; 74:9–10; 79:5; 80:4; 89:4; 90:13; 94:3. See also Zech. 1:12.

42. David Aune, *Revelation 6–16*, vol 52b of Word Biblical Commentary (Dallas: Word Books, 1998), 406.

43. JoAnn Marie Terrell, *Power in the Blood? The Cross in the African American Experience* (Maryknoll, NY: Orbis Books, 1998), 74.

44. Pinn, *Terror and Triumph*, 84.

45. Terrell, *Power in the Blood?* 49.

46. Pinn, *Terror and Triumph*, 99.

47. Of course, the response expected of God in this text has often been categorized as unchristian because of the heavy expectation that when God acts God may well do so violently. Clearly, the souls cry out for God's intervention, and the language of both judgment and vengeance is used. Even

though John never counsels his witnesses to witness violently, it is clear that God is caught up in a contest of lethal cosmic force. Many scholars are quick to point out, however, that the violence so addressed is violence in the realm of public justice, not private vengeance: G. B. Caird, *The Revelation of St. John the Divine* (San Francisco: Harper & Row, 1966), 85; G. K. Beale, *The Book of Revelation: A Commentary on the Greek Text* (Grand Rapids: Wm. B. Eerdmans Publishing Co., 1999), 392. Caird even notes that the language is symbolically appropriate to the witness context; the justice John describes is legal justice: "The martyr has been condemned in a human court of law, and the decision stands against them unless it is reversed in a higher court. But the heavenly judge cannot declare them to be in the right without at the same time declaring their persecutors to be in the wrong and passing sentence against them. Justice must not only be done; it must be seen to be done" (Caird, *Revelation*, 85). And in a case where the force representing Satan, Rome, will fight with violence, John apparently thought that, if cosmic and historical justice were to be served, God would need to respond in kind. This expectation of violence to bring about justice is, of course, a long-held Old Testament theological understanding. While pointing most specifically to the imprecatory psalms (Pss. 7, 35, 55, 58, 59, 69, 79, 83, 109, 137, 139), Aune also notes that there are large swathes of Old Testament and other Jewish materials that indicate God's need and right to respond appropriately to human violence (Aune, *Revelation 6–16*, 407–11). Lincoln and Mamiya point out that Christians in the Black Church tradition have long identified with this Old Testament view of God: "the Old Testament notion of God as an avenging, conquering, liberating paladin remains a formidable anchor of the faith in most black churches" (Lincoln and Mamiya, *The Black Church*, 3). Speaking from the black church tradition in South Africa, Boesak even challenges that in denying this reality, white Christians not only desecrate the faith, but also do so in a way that helps perpetuate the very evils their Christian God supposedly deplores: "Why is there this division between the God of the Old Testament and the God of Jesus? Why, on this point, does white Western Christianity go back to the heresy of Marcionism? God takes up the cause of the poor and the oppressed precisely because in this world their voices are not heard—not even by those who call themselves Christians. God even has to take up the cause of the poor *against* 'Christians.' Christians who enjoy the fruits of injustice without a murmur, who remain silent as the defenseless are slaughtered, dare not become indignant when the suffering people of God echo the prayers of the psalms and pray for deliverance and judgment" (Allan A. Boesak, *Comfort and Protest: The Apocalypse from a South African Perspective* [Philadelphia: Westminster Press, 1987], 72–73). To be sure, this was certainly the perspective of African Americans both slave and free, prior to the dawning of the Civil War, whose coming they envisioned as God's march towards a justice too long delayed.

128   *Notes*

And so Pinn can conclude that "this was also the attitude of many blacks during the Civil War because it was theologically presented as a just war through which redemption would occur, if leaders were obedient to the leanings of God" (Pinn, *Why, Lord?* 91).

48. J. P. Heil, "The Fifth Seal (Rev 6, 9–11) as a Key to the Book of Revelation," *Biblica* 74 (1993): 231–32.
49. Pinn, *Terror and Triumph*, 96.
50. Ibid., 97.
51. Ibid.
52. Ibid., 143.
53. Cf. 6:11. Although the Greek says literally, "until their fellow servants and brothers should be fulfilled," I take the *and* (*kai*) that connects the two nouns to be epexegetical. I therefore translate, "until the number of their fellow servants, who are their brothers . . ." See also 1:9, where John describes himself as a fellow worker and brother with an epexegetical *kai*. Clearly there, since he is referring to himself, he cannot be designating two different people. The same construction and interpretation follow here.
54. Aune, *Revelation 6–16*, 391.
55. Reddish, *Revelation*, 131.
56. Gerhard Delling, "πλήρης, πληρόω," *TDNT* 6, no 283–311: 297.
57. Pinn, *Terror and Triumph*, 154.
58. Since *word* and *witness* are equivalent, it doesn't matter that John mentions *word* first at 6:9 and *witness* first at 20:4.
59. David Aune, *Revelation 17–22*, vol 52c of Word Biblical Commentary (Dallas: Word Books, 1997), 1085.
60. Ibid., 1088.
61. Cf. Reddish, *Revelation*, 382. Reddish points out that it is not entirely clear on first sight who actually occupies the thrones here in 20:4. However, after careful grammatical consideration, he concludes that the occupants are the same souls who have been beheaded. "The word 'and' (Greek: *kai*) is best understood as an epexegetic or explanatory use of *kai*; that is, the souls of the ones beheaded are the ones he saw seated on the thrones." See also Aune, *Revelation 17–22*, 1084–85.
62. Cf. Fiorenza, *Vision of a Just World*, 108: "The phrase 'come to life again' does not connote in Revelation a spiritual or a limited resurrection since it refers in 2:8 to the resurrection of Christ and in 13:14 to that of the beast's heads. . . . Rather, this vision of the millennium speaks about the final resurrection of those Christians who have died in their resistance to the imperial cult and have remained loyal to God and the Lamb. Because they have ratified their baptism with their life-praxis (1:6; 5:10), they assume the eschatological reign as priests."
63. William H. Shea, "The Parallel Literary Structure of Revelation 12 and 20," *Andrews University Seminary Studies* 23 (1985): 37–54.

64. Shea, "Revelation 12 and 20," 43: "That being the case, Rev 20:3 and 20:7 stand in the same position in their narrative as do Rev 12:6 and 12:13–16 in theirs."
65. Shea, "Revelation 12 and 20," 46.
66. See, for example, Dorothy A. Lee, "The Heavenly Woman and the Dragon: ReReadings of Revelation 12," in *Feminist Poetics of the Sacred: Creative Suspicions*, ed. Frances Devlin-Glass and Lyn McCredden (Oxford: Oxford University Press, 2001), 198–220; Aune, *Revelation 6–16*, 658–703; Reddish, *Revelation*, 232; Pablo Richard, *Apocalypse: A People's Commentary on the Book of Revelation* (Maryknoll, NY: Orbis Books, 1995), 102.
67. Reddish, *Revelation*, 230.
68. Cf. Aune, *Revelation 6–16*, 658.
69. Cf. Reddish, *Revelation*, 121: "In attempting to understand John's vision, the reader must avoid a rigid, chronological interpretation of the imagery of Revelation."
70. While not positing that chapter 12 is a flashback, scholars have recognized that the chapter, along with the following chapters 13 and 14, does represent a break in the movement of John's narration. See, for example, J. Lambrecht, "The Opening of the Seals (Rev 6,1–8,6)," *Biblica* 79 (1998): 218: "The materials of chapters 12–13 and 14 are best seen as intercalations *vis-à-vis* the main 'seven' structure suggested by the opening of the scroll"; Reddish, *Revelation*, 229: "Viewed in the light of the overall structure of the Apocalypse, 12:1–14:20 functions as a break in the action, a pause to present a close look at the assault on the people of God by the forces of evil."
71. Aune, *Revelation 6–16*, 676.
72. Cf., Reddish, *Revelation*, 235–36.
73. Lee, "The Heavenly Woman and the Dragon," 201.
74. Richard, *Apocalypse*, 100–101.
75. Boesak, *Comfort and Protest*, 86–88.
76. Ibid., 88.
77. Pinn, *The Black Church*, xiv.
78. Paris, *Social Teaching*, 3.
79. James Weldon Johnson and J. Rosamond Johnson, *The Books of American Negro Spirituals* (New York: Viking Press, 1969), 130–33.

Chapter 3: Wreaking Weakness

1. See also connections to the blood of the lamb at 7:24; 12:11.
2. Cf. 5:6 (throne), 8 (throne context, v. 9), 12 (at the throne), 13 (throne); 6:1, 16 (throne); 7:9 (throne), 10 (throne), 14 (at the throne), 17 (throne); 12:11; 13:8, 11; 14:1, 4, 10; 15:3; 17:14.
3. The term *lamb*, greek *arnion*, occurs twenty-seven times in Revelation overall. On eleven occasions, it occurs with or in direct relationship to the throne. On nine occasions it occurs at or after 19:7, when the Lamb is victoriously

described as the bridegroom of the new Jerusalem. The final two such occur-rences, 22:1 and 22:3, occur in those victorious later chapters and are thus not figured into the combat scene equations.

4. Cf. 19:7, 9; 21:9, 14, 22, 23, 27; 22:1, 3.
5. Cf. David Aune, "Following the Lamb: Discipleship in the Apocalypse," in *Patterns of Discipleship in the New Testament*, ed. Richard N. Longenecker (Grand Rapids: Wm. B. Eerdmans Publishing Co., 1996), 278: "The victory achieved by Jesus through suffering and death becomes a central paradigm for discipleship in the Apocalypse."
6. JoAnn Marie Terrell, *Power in the Blood? The Cross in the African American Experience* (Maryknoll, NY: Orbis Books, 1998), 37.
7. Anthony B. Pinn, *Why, Lord? Suffering and Evil in Black Theology* (New York: Continuum, 1995), 15.
8. Terrell, *Power in the Blood?* 52.
9. Quoted in Terrell, *Power in the Blood?* 10, from the poem *On Being Brought from Africa to America (1768)*.
10. Terrell, *Power in the Blood?* 75.
11. Pinn, *Why, Lord?* 9.
12. Ibid., 17.
13. Terrell, *Power in the Blood?* 7.
14. Cf., 1:5; 5:9; 7:14; 12:11; 19:13.
15. Terrell, *Power in the Blood?* 6–7.
16. Pinn, *Why, Lord?* 10–11.
17. Ibid., 18.
18. Ibid.
19. Ibid., 157.
20. Terrell, *Power in the Blood?* 45.
21. Pinn, *Why, Lord?* 158.
22. Delores Williams, "A Crucifixion Double Cross?" *Other Side* 29, no. 5 (September–October 1993): 27.
23. Loren Johns, *The Lamb Christology of the Apocalypse of John* (Tübingen: Mohr-Siebeck, 2003), 106.
24. Ibid., 129.
25. Ibid.
26. Ibid., 130.
27. Cf. Johns, *Lamb Christology*, 106, 145–49.
28. Johns, *Lamb Christology*, 148.
29. Theophus Smith, *Conjuring Culture: Biblical Formations of Black America* (New York and Oxford: Oxford University Press, 1994), 164.
30. Ibid., 168.
31. Ibid., 226.
32. Ibid., 169.
33. Ibid., 226.

34. See René Girard, *Violence and the Sacred*, trans. Patrick Gregory (Baltimore: Johns Hopkins University Press, 1977), and *The Scapegoat*, trans. Yvonne Frecerro (Baltimore: Johns Hopkins University Press, 1986).

35. Cf. Johns, *Lamb Christology*, 201–2: "As demonstrated above, there is little in the Apocalypse of John to support an understanding of Jesus' death as 'sacrificial' in the substitutionary or penal sense."

36. Smith, *Conjuring Culture*, 199.

37. Johns, *Lamb Christology*, 161.

38. Ibid., 173–74.

39. Ibid., 161.

40. Smith, *Conjuring Culture*, 213.

41. Quoted in Pinn, *Why, Lord?* 75–76. Martin Luther King Jr., Untitled Montgomery Improvement Association Address, 1959, Boston University, King Collection, Box 2, 1–11, Folder 2.

42. Quoted in Pinn, *Why, Lord?* 76. From "Suffering and Faith," in *A Testament of Hope: The Essential Writings of Martin Luther King Jr.*, ed. James Washington (San Francisco: Harper & Row, 1986), 41.

43. Quoted in Pinn, *Why, Lord?* 76. In "Shattered Dreams," Boston University King Collection, Box 119 a. XVI. 16, 10.

44. Smith, *Conjuring Culture*, 183 (italics mine).

45. James Cone, *Martin & Malcolm & America: A Dream or a Nightmare* (Maryknoll, NY: Orbis Books, 1991).

46. Pinn, *Why, Lord?* 76–77.

47. Quoted in Pinn, *Why, Lord?* 77. See Martin Luther King Jr., *Where Do We Go from Here: Chaos or Community* (Boston: Beacon Press, 1967), 37.

48. Patricia M. McDonald, "Lion as Slain Lamb: On Reading Revelation Recursively," *Horizons* 23, no 1 (1996): 33. See also Richard Bauckham, *The Climax of Prophecy: Studies on the Book of Revelation* (Edinburgh: T. & T. Clark, 1993), 183: "Jesus Christ *is* the Lion of Judah and the Root of David, but John 'sees' him as the Lamb. Precisely by juxtaposing these contrasting images, John forges a symbol of conquest by sacrificial death, which is essentially a new symbol."

49. Robert H. Mounce, "Worthy Is the Lamb," in *Scripture, Tradition, and Interpretation: Essays Presented to Everett F. Harrison by His Students and Colleagues in Honor of His Seventy-fifth Birthday*, ed. W. Ward Gasque and William Sanford LaSor (Grand Rapids: Wm. B. Eerdmans Publishing Co., 1978), 68.

50. McDonald, "Lion as Slain Lamb," 37.

51. Indeed, this lion also *slaughtered Lambs* God's people. Jesus' death on the cross, after all, is as much a judgment as it is a victory. That is a point John tries desperately to get across in his chapter 2 and 3 letters to his wavering churches.

52. Johns, *Lamb Christology*, 122. Johns points to 2:10–11; 7:13–14; 11:7–9; 12:11; 16:6; 17:6; 18:24; 19:2; 20:4–6).

53. Johns, *Lamb Christology*, 127.
54. Ibid.

Chapter 4: The Rap against Rome

1. Loren Johns, *The Lamb Christology of the Apocalypse of John* (Tübingen: Mohr-Siebeck, 2003), 152.
2. Elisabeth Schüssler Fiorenza, *The Book of Revelation: Justice and Judgment* (Minneapolis: Fortress Press, 1998), 166.
3. Cornel West, "On Afro-American Popular Music: From Bebop to Rap," *Black Sacred Music: A Journal of Theomusicology* 6, no 1 (1992): 291. See also James H. Cone, *The Spirituals and the Blues* (Maryknoll, NY: Orbis Books, 1972); James H. Cone, "The Blues: A Secular Spiritual," *Black Sacred Music: A Journal of Theomusicology* 6, no 1 (1992): 68–97.
4. West, "On Afro-American Popular Music," 282.
5. Ibid., 291.
6. See Brian K. Blount, *Cultural Interpretation: Reorienting New Testament Criticism* (Minneapolis: Fortress Press, 1995).
7. Cone, *The Spirituals and the Blues*, 31.
8. Cone, "The Blues," 73.
9. Ibid.
10. Larry Neal, "The Ethos of the Blues," *Black Sacred Music: A Journal of Theomusicology* 6, no 1 (1992): 41.
11. Cone, "The Blues," 71.
12. Cf. Anthony B. Pinn, *Why, Lord? Suffering and Evil in Black Theology* (New York: Continuum, 1995), 119.
13. Teresa L. Reed, *The Holy Profane: Religion in Black Popular Music* (Lexington: University Press of Kentucky, 2003), 39.
14. Ibid., 40–41.
15. Quoted in Reed, *The Holy Profane*, 41.
16. Cone, "The Blues," 85. See also Pinn, *Why, Lord?* 118: "Within these songs [blues], the promises of the spirituals were weighed and tested in light of life's controlling hardships, and utopian ideals were found wanting. Hence, the blues as a musical form is concerned with truth as it arises out of experience."
17. Neal, "The Ethos of the Blues," 3.
18. Anthony B. Pinn, *The Black Church in the Post–Civil Rights Era* (Maryknoll, NY: Orbis Books, 2002), 52.
19. Reed, *The Holy Profane*, 11.
20. Pinn, *The Black Church*, 48.
21. Ibid., 47–48.
22. C. Eric Lincoln and Lawrence H. Mamiya, *The Black Church in the African American Experience* (Durham and London: Duke University Press, 1990), 369: "Some freedom songs were composed specifically for the civil rights

movement, while most were adaptations of extant songs—in this case, spirituals and gospels."

23. Cf. Lincoln and Mamiya, *The Black Church*, 369.
24. West, "On Afro-American Popular Music," 292.
25. Pinn, *Why, Lord?* 121–22.
26. Michael Eric Dyson, "Performance, Protest, and Prophecy in the Culture of Hip-Hop," *Black Sacred Music: A Journal of Theomusicology* 5, no 1 (1991): 18.
27. West, "On Afro-American Popular Music," 292; ibid., 12–13.
28. Dyson, "Performance, Protest, and Prophecy," 14.
29. West, "On Afro-American Popular Music," 293.
30. Dyson, "Performance, Protest, and Prophecy," 13.
31. Pinn, *Why, Lord?* 122.
32. Michael Eric Dyson, "Rap Culture, the Church, and American Society," *Black Sacred Music: A Journal of Theomusicology* 6, no 1 (1992): 272.
33. Quoted in Dyson, "Performance, Protest, and Prophecy," 23.
34. Quoted in Dyson, "Performance, Protest, and Prophecy," 14.
35. For a descriptive classification of rap into "status," "gangsta," and "progressive" categories, see Pinn, *Why, Lord?* 125–33. The qualities of "progressive rap" have been the positive characteristics of the genre noted thus far.
36. West, "On Afro-American Popular Music," 293.
37. The threefold pattern, "Holy, holy, holy," is inspired by the Trisagion of Isa. 6:3.
38. For the threefold formula, "who was, who is, and who will be," as related to Greco-Roman mythology, see M. Eugene Boring, *Revelation* (Louisville, Ky.: Westminster John Knox Press, 1989), 75.
39. Cf. David Aune, *Revelation 6–16*, vol 52b of Word Biblical Commentary (Dallas: Word Books, 1998), 642: "The phrase *kurie ho theos ho pantokratōr*, 'Lord God Almighty,' is a formula found five times in Revelation (4:8; 11:17; 15:3; 16:7; 21:22). . . . It is particularly significant that the full title occurs in Revelation several times in close association with the title . . . 'who was and is (and is to come)': 1:8; 4:8; 11:17."
40. Cf. G. K. Beale, *The Book of Revelation: A Commentary on the Greek Text* (Grand Rapids: Wm. B. Eerdmans Publishing Co., 1999), 334–35. "That such a contrast between God's eternal kingship and that of the temporal rulers is meant in v. 10 is apparent from the striking similarity of the divine title 'the Lord and our God' in v. 11a to the title *dominus et deus noster* used to address the emperor Domitian (so Suetonius, *Dom.* 13)." See also Catherine Gonzalez and Justo L. Gonzalez, *The Book of Revelation* (Louisville, Ky.: Westminster John Knox, 1997), 40–41: "There are clearly political connotations to this scene of the twenty-four elders casting their crowns. When Tiridates, a king from that area, wished to show his obeisance to Roman emperor Nero, he did so by placing his crown at Nero's feet."

41. A   4:8   5:14   Four Creatures (Cherubim) Praise
    B   4:9   5:12–13   Glory, Thanks (4:9), Honor, Power (5:12–13)
    C   4:10 5:11   Worship
    B* 4:10 5:10   Crowns/Kingdom
    A* 4:11 5:9   Worthy
42. Elisabeth Schüssler Fiorenza, *Revelation: Vision of a Just World* (Minneapolis: Fortress Press, 1991), 61.
43. Cf. Aune, *Revelation 6–16*, 468–69. Citing 2 Macc. 14:4, he points to an ex-priest named Alcimus, who gave the Syrian King Demetrius I Soter (187–150 BCE) a gold crown and a palm, which were most likely symbols of a victorious ruler. Similar gifts were given with the same probable effect to Demetrius II Nicator (161–125 BCE) by Simon the Hasmonean (1 Macc. 13:36–37).
44. Aune, *Revelation 6–16*, 469.
45. Boring, *Revelation*, 192.
46. Cf. Beale, *Revelation*, 818. Beale notices the intentional connections between this hymnic unit and the narration about the slaughtered souls beneath the altar following the opening of the fifth seal at 6:9–11. He points out that the hymnic use of *the Holy One* (*ho hosios*) and *judge* (*krinō*) "reflects virtually the same description of God in 6:10, which is the persecuted saints' prayer to God that he will vindicate himself and them by judging their persecutors."
47. Cf. Mitchell G. Reddish, *Revelation* (Macon, GA: Smyth & Helwys, 2001), 360. For background discussion of Hallelujah as related to the Hallel Psalms (113–18) and Psalm 104:35, see Beale, *Revelation*, 926–30.
48. Boring, *Revelation*, 192.
49. Ibid., 193.
50. Beale, *Revelation*, 939.
51. Ibid.
52. Cf. Boring, *Revelation*, 173: "John has often used the Exodus story as a model for God's eschatological deliverance from the oppressive 'Egypt' of his own day. This section (15:1–16:21) represents his most thorough use of this motif in Revelation." See also Beale, *Revelation*, 794: "The actual contents of the song itself come not from Exodus 15 but from passages throughout the OT extolling God's character."
53. Boring, *Revelation*, 173.
54. Lincoln and Mamiya, *The Black Church*, 348.
55. Cone, "The Blues," 69.
56. Schüssler Fiorenza, *Vision of a Just World*, 129.
57. Cf. Cone, "The Blues," 78, who notes that even the blues, the most likely of the forms to lack a historical component, has strong ties to the African American past and uses those ties in its musical presentations. He states simply: "Because the blues are rooted in the black perception of existence, they are historical."

58. Dyson, "Rap Culture," 272. See also Dyson, "Performance, Protest, and Prophecy," 22: "It is also refreshing to watch hip-hop culture revive an explicit historicism that combats the amnesia threatening to further consign the measured achievements of the recent black past into disabling lapses of memory. Hip-hop has infused a revived sense of historical pride into young black minds that is salutary insofar as it provides a solid base for self-esteem."

59. David Aune, *Revelation 1–5*, vol 52a of Word Biblical Commentary (Dallas: Word Books, 1997), 315–16.

60. Reed, *The Holy Profane*, 43.

61. Reddish, *Revelation*, 298.

62. Aune, *Revelation 1–5*, 316.

63. Aune, *Revelation 1–5*, 316. See also Aune, *Revelation 1–5*, 308–14; Boring, *Revelation*, 192.

64. Schüssler Fiorenza, *Vision of a Just World*, 102.

65. Reed, *The Holy Profane*, 153–54.

66. Ibid., 155.

67. Ibid., 156.

68. Ibid., 160.

69. Pinn, *Why, Lord?* 128.

70. Dyson, "Rap Culture," 273.

71. Pinn, *Why, Lord?* 117.

Bibliography

Andrews, Dwight D. "From Black to Blue." *Black Sacred Music: A Journal of Theo-musicology* 6, no. 1 (1992): 47–54.

Aune, David. "Following the Lamb: Discipleship in the Apocalypse." In *Patterns of Discipleship in the New Testament*, edited by Richard N. Longenecker, 269–84. Grand Rapids: Wm. B. Eerdmans Publishing Co., 1996.

———. *Revelation 1–5.* Vol. 52a of Word Biblical Commentary. Dallas: Word Books, 1997.

———. *Revelation 17–22.* Vol. 52c of Word Biblical Commentary. Dallas: Word Books, 1997.

———. *Revelation 6–16.* Vol. 52b of Word Biblical Commentary. Dallas: Word Books, 1998.

Aus, Roger D. "The Relevance of Isaiah 66:7 to Revelation 12 and 2 Thessalonians 1." *Zeitschrift für die Neutestamentliche Wissenschaft und die Kunde der Alteren Kirche* 67 (1976): 252–68.

Bach, Alice. "On the Road between Birmingham and Jerusalem." Semeia 82 (1998): 297–305.

Bailey, Randall C., ed. *Yet With A Steady Beat: Contemporary U.S. Afrocentric Biblical Interpretation.* Atlanta: Society of Biblical Literature, 2003.

Bailey, Wilma Ann. "The Sorrow Songs: Laments from Ancient Israel and the African American Diaspora." *Semeia Studies* 42 (2003), 61–83.

Barr, David L. "Towards an Ethical Reading of the Apocalypse: Reflections on John's Use of Power, Violence, and Misogyny." In *Society of Biblical Literature 1997 Seminar Papers*, 358–73. Atlanta: Scholars Press, 1997.

Bauckham, Richard. *The Climax of Prophecy: Studies on the Book of Revelation.* Edinburgh: T. & T. Clark, 1993.

———. *The Theology of the Book of Revelation.* Cambridge: Cambridge University Press, 1993.

Beale, G. K. *The Book of Revelation: A Commentary on the Greek Text.* Grand Rapids: Wm. B. Eerdmans Publishing Co., 1999.

Bertram, Georg. "ψυχή. . . ." *TDNT* 9: 608–66.

Billingsley, Andrew. *Mighty Like a River: The Black Church and Social Reform.* New York and Oxford: Oxford University Press, 1999.

Blassingame, John W., ed. *Slave Testimony: Two Centuries of Letters, Speeches, Interviews, and Autobiographies.* Baton Rouge: Louisana State University Press, 1977.

Blount, Brian K. *Cultural Interpretation: Reorienting New Testament Criticism.* Minneapolis: Fortress Press, 1995.

———. "If You Get MY Meaning: Introducing Cultural Exegesis." In *Exegese und Theoriediskussion,* edited by Stefan Alkier and Ralph Brucker, 77–97. Tübingen and Basel: Francke-Verlag, 1998.

———. "Reading Revelation Today: Witness as Active Resistance." *Interpretation* 54 (2000): 398–412.

———. *Then the Whisper Put On Flesh: New Testament Ethics in an African American Context.* Nashville: Abingdon Press, 2001.

Boesak, Allan A. *Comfort and Protest: The Apocalypse from a South African Perspective.* Philadelphia: Westminister Press, 1987.

Boring, M. Eugene. *Revelation.* Louisville, Ky.: John Knox Press, 1989.

Brasher, Brenda E. "From Revelation to the X-Files: An Autopsy of Millennialism in American Popular Culture." *Semeia* 82 (1998): 281–95.

Brett, Mark G. "Interpreting Ethnicity: Method, Hermeneutics, Ethics." In *Ethnicity and the Bible,* edited by Mark G. Brett, 3–22. Leiden and New York: E. J. Brill, 1996.

Broadbent, Ralph. "Ideology, Culture, and British New Testament Studies: The Challenge of Cultural Studies." *Semeia* 82 (1998): 33–61.

Caird, G. B. *The Revelation of St. John the Divine.* San Francisco: Harper & Row, 1966.

Caldwell, Larry. "Third Horizon Ethnohermeneutics: Re-evaluating New Testament Hermeneutical Models for Intercultural Biblical Interpreters Today." *Asia Journal of Theology* 1 (1987): 314–33.

Collins, Adela Yarbro. *Crisis and Catharsis: The Power of the Apocalypse.* Philadelphia: Westminster Press, 1984.

———. "The Political Perspective of the Revelation to John." *Journal of Biblical Literature* 96 (1977): 241–56.

Cone, James H. "The Blues: A Secular Spiritual." *Black Sacred Music: A Journal of Theomusicology* 6, no. 1 (1992): 68–97.

———. *Martin & Malcolm & America: A Dream or a Nightmare.* Maryknoll, NY: Orbis Books, 1991.

———. *Risks of Faith: The Emergence of a Black Theology of Liberation, 1968–1998.* Boston: Beacon Press, 1999.

———. *The Spirituals and the Blues.* Maryknoll, NY: Orbis Books, 1972.

Craffert, Pieter F. "On New Testament Interpretation and Ethnocentrism." In *Ethnicity and the Bible*, edited by Mark G. Brett, 449–68. Leiden and New York: E. J. Brill, 1996.

Delling, Gerhard. "πλήρης, πληρόω. . . ." *TDNT* 6, no. 283–311.

Donaldson, Laura E. "Are We All Multiculturists Now? Biblical Reading as Cultural Contact." *Semeia* 82 (1998): 79–97.

Dube, Musa W. "Consuming a Colonial Cultural Bomb: Translating *Badimo* into 'Demons' in the Setswana Bible." *JSNT* 73 (1999): 33–59.

During, Simon, ed. *The Cultural Studies Reader.* London and New York: Routledge Press, 1999.

Dyson, Michael Eric. "Performance, Protest, and Prophecy in the Culture of Hip-Hop." *Black Sacred Music: A Journal of Theomusicology* 5, no. 1 (1991): 12–24.

———. "Rap Culture, the Church, and American Society." *Black Sacred Music: A Journal of Theomusicology* 6, no. 1 (1992): 268–73.

Ellingworth, Paul. "Understanding and Applying the Bible Today." In *The Bible in Cultural Context*, edited by Helena Pavlincová and Dalibor Papoušek, 113–24. Brno: Czech Society for the Study of Religions, 1994.

Exum, J. Cheryl, and Stephen D. Moore, eds. *Biblical Studies/Cultural Studies: The Third Sheffield Colloquium.* Sheffield: Sheffield Academic Press, 1998.

———. "Biblical Studies/Cultural Studies." In *Biblical Studies/Cultural Studies: The Third Sheffield Colloquium*, edited by J. Cheryl Exum and Stephen D. Moore, 19–45. Sheffield: Sheffield Academic Press, 1998.

Fiorenza, Elisabeth Schüssler. *The Book of Revelation: Justice and Judgment.* Minneapolis: Fortress Press, 1998.

———. "The Followers of the Lamb: Visionary Rhetoric and Social-Political Situation." *Semeia* 36 (1986): 123–46.

———. *Revelation: Vision of a Just World.* Minneapolis: Fortress Press, 1991.

Fiske, John. "Cultural Studies and the Culture of Everyday Life." In *Cultural Studies*, edited by Lawrence Grossberg, Cary Nelson, and Paula A. Treichler, 154–65. New York and London: Routledge Press, 1992.

Gilroy, Paul. "Cultural Studies and Ethnic Absolutism." In *Cultural Studies*, edited by Lawrence Grossberg, Cary Nelson, and Paula A. Treichler, 187–98. New York and London: Routledge Press, 1992.

Glancy, Jennifer A. "Text Appeal: Visual Pleasure and Biblical Studies." *Semeia* 82 (1998): 63–78.

Gonzalez, Catherine, and Justo L. Gonzalez. *The Book of Revelation.* Louisville, Ky.: Westminster John Knox Press, 1997.

Griffiths, Richard. "Mrs. Thatcher's Bible." *Semeia* 82 (1998): 99–125.

Grossberg, Lawrence, Cary Nelson, and Paula A. Treichler, eds. *Cultural Studies.* New York and London: Routledge Press, 1992.

Gruenwald, Ithamar. "A Case Study of Scripture and Culture: Apocalypticism as Cultural Identity in Past and Present." In *Ancient and Modern Perspectives on the Bible and Culture: Essays in Honor of Hans Dieter Betz*, edited by Adela Yarbro Collins, 252–80. Atlanta: Scholars Press, 1998.

Gruver, Rod. "The Blues as a Secular Religion." *Black Sacred Music: A Journal of Theomusicology* 6, no. 1 (1992): 55–67.

Hall, Stuart. "Cultural Studies and Its Theoretical Legacies." In *Cultural Studies*, edited by Lawrence Grossberg, Cary Nelson, and Paula A. Treichler, 277–86. New York and London: Routledge Press, 1992.

———. "Cultural Studies: Two Paradigms." In *What Is Cultural Studies? A Reader*, edited by John Storey, 31–48. London: Arnold Press, 1996.

Harris, Frederick C. *Something Within: Religion in African-American Political Activism*. New York and Oxford: Oxford University Press, 1999.

Heil, J. P. "The Fifth Seal (Rev 6, 9–11) as a Key to the Book of Revelation." *Biblica* 74 (1993): 220–43.

Hopkins, Dwight N. *Down, Up, and Over: Slave Religion and Black Theology*. Minneapolis: Fortress Press, 1999.

Horn, Stephen Norwood. "The Author's Use of Hymns as Summaries of the Theology of the Book of Revelation." New Orleans: New Orleans Baptist Theological Seminary, 1998.

Johns, Loren. *The Lamb Christology of the Apocalypse of John*. Tübingen: Mohr-Siebeck, 2003.

Johnson, James Weldon, and J. Rosamond Johnson. *The Books of American Negro Spirituals*. New York: Viking Press, 1969.

Kampen, John. "The Genre and Function of Apocalyptic Literature in the African American Experience." In *Text and Experience: Towards A Cultural Exegesis of the Bible*, edited by Daniel Smith-Christopher, 43–65. Sheffield: Sheffield Academic Press, 1995.

Keller, Catherine. *Apocalypse Now and Then: A Feminist Guide to the End of the World*. Boston: Beacon Press, 1996.

Kim, Jean K. "'Uncovering Her Wickedness': An Inter(con)Textual Reading of Revelation 17 from Postcolonial Feminist Perspective." *JSNT* 73 (1999): 61–81.

Kirk-Duggan, Cheryl. *Exorcising Evil: A Womanist Perspective on the Spirituals*. Maryknoll, NY: Orbis Books, 1997.

Lambrecht, J. "The Opening of the Seals (Rev 6,1–8,6)." *Biblica* 79 (1998): 198–220.

Lee, Dorothy A. "The Heavenly Woman and the Dragon: ReReadings of Revelation 12." In *Feminist Poetics of the Sacred: Creative Suspicions*, edited by Frances Devlin-Glass and Lyn McCredden, 198–220. Oxford: Oxford University Press, 2001.

Lenchak, Timothy. "The Bible and Intercultural Communication." *Missiology: An International Review* 22 (1994): 457–68.

Liew, Tat-siong Benny. "Tyranny, Boundary, and Might: Colonial Mimicry in Mark's Gospel." *JSNT* 73 (1999): 7–31.

Lincoln, C. Eric, and Lawrence H. Mamiya. *The Black Church in the African American Experience*. Durham and London: Duke University Press, 1990.

Mabee, Charles. *Reading Sacred Texts through American Eyes: Biblical Interpretation as Cultural Critique*. Macon, GA: Mercer University Press, 1991.

MacLeod, David J. "The Fourth 'Last Thing': The Millennial Kingdom of Christ (Rev. 20:4–6)." *Bibliotheca Sacra* 157 (2000): 44–67.

Mazzaferri, Fred. "MARTYRIA IĒSOU Revisited." *Bible Translator* 39 (1988): 114–22.

McDonald, Patricia M. "Lion as Slain Lamb: On Reading Revelation Recursively." *Horizons* 23, no. 1 (1996): 29–47.

McRobbie, Angela. "Post-Marxism and Cultural Studies: A Postscript." In *Cultural Studies*, edited by Lawrence Grossberg, Cary Nelson, and Paula A. Treichler, 719–30. New York and London: Routledge Press, 1992.

Michel, Otto. "σφάζω, σφαγή. . . ." *TDNT* 7: 925–38.

Moore, Stephen D. "Between Birmingham and Jerusalem: Cultural Studies and Biblical Studies." *Semeia* 82 (1998): 1–32.

———, ed. *In Search of the Present: The Bible through Cultural Studies*. Semeia 82. Atlanta: SBL, 1998.

———. "Introduction." *Semeia* 82 (1998): vii–viii.

———. "Ugly Thoughts: On the Face and Physique of the Historical Jesus." In *Biblical Studies/Cultural Studies: The Third Sheffield Colloquium*, edited by J. Cheryl Exum and Stephen D. Moore, 376–99. Sheffield: Sheffield Academic Press, 1998.

Mounce, Robert H. *The Book of Revelation*. 2nd edition. Grand Rapids: Wm. B. Eerdmans Publishing Co., 1998.

———. "Worthy Is the Lamb." In *Scripture, Tradition, and Interpretation: Essays Presented to Everett F. Harrison by His Students and Colleagues in Honor of His Seventy-fifth Birthday*, edited by W. Ward Gasque and William Sanford LaSor, 60–69. Grand Rapids: Wm. B. Eerdmans Publishing Co., 1978.

Nash, Peter Theodore. "Cross-Cultural Reading of the Bible." *Word and World* 13, no. 4 (1993): 398–401.

Neal, Larry. "The Ethos of the Blues." *Black Sacred Music: A Journal of Theomusicology* 6, no. 1 (1992): 36–46.

Nelson, Cary, Lawrence Grossberg, and Paula A. Treichler. "Cultural Studies: An Introduction." In *Cultural Studies*, edited by Lawrence Grossberg, Cary Nelson, and Paula A. Treichler, 1–16. New York and London: Routledge Press, 1992.

O'Connor, Alan. "The Problem of American Cultural Studies." In *What Is Cultural Studies? A Reader*, edited by John Storey, 187–96. London: Arnold Press, 1996.

O'Rourke, John. "The Hymns of the Apocalypse." *CBQ* 30 (1968): 399–409.

Paris, Peter J. *The Social Teaching of the Black Churches*. Philadelphia: Fortress Press, 1985.

Pfister, Joel. "The Americanization of Cultural Studies." In *What Is Cultural Studies? A Reader*, edited by John Storey, 287–99. London: Arnold Press, 1996.

Pinn, Anthony B. *The Black Church in the Post–Civil Rights Era*. Maryknoll, NY: Orbis Books, 2002.

———. "Rap Music and Its Message: On Interpreting the Contact between Religion and Popular Culture." In *Religion and Popular Culture in America*, edited by Bruce David Forbes and Jeffrey H. Mahan, 258–75. Berkeley: University of California Press, 2002.

———. *Terror and Triumph: The Nature of Black Religion*. Minneapolis: Fortress Press, 2003.

———. *Why, Lord? Suffering and Evil in Black Theology*. New York: Continuum, 1995.

Pippin, Tina. *Death and Desire: The Rhetoric of Gender in the Apocalypse of John*. Louisville, Ky.: Westminster John Knox Press, 1992.

Reddish, Mitchell G. *Revelation*. Macon, GA: Smyth & Helwys, 2001.

Reed, Teresa L. *The Holy Profane: Religion in Black Popular Music*. Lexington: University Press of Kentucky, 2003.

Richard, Pablo. *Apocalypse: A People's Commentary on the Book of Revelation*. Maryknoll, NY: Orbis Books, 1995.

Rowland, Christopher. "The Lamb and the Beast, the Sheep and the Goats: 'The Mystery of Salvation' in Revelation." In *A Vision for the Church: Studies in Early Christian Ecclesiology in Honour of J. P. M. Sweet*, edited by Markus Bockmuehl and Michael B. Thompson, 181–91. Edinburgh: T. & T. Clark, 1997.

Ruiz, Jean Pierre. "Revelation 4:8–11; 5:9–14: Hymns of the Heavenly Liturgy." *Society of Biblical Literature Seminar Papers* 34 (1995): 216–20.

Segovia, Fernando F. *Decolonizing Biblical Studies: A View from the Margins*. Maryknoll, NY: Orbis Books, 2000.

———. "Racial and Ethnic Minorities in Biblical Studies." In *Ethnicity and the Bible*, edited by Mark G. Brett, 469–92. Leiden and New York: E. J. Brill, 1996.

———. "Toward a Hermeneutic of the Diaspora: A Hermeneutics of Otherness and Engagement." In *Reading from This Place: Social Location and Biblical Interpretation in the United States*, edited by Fernando F. Segovia and Mary Ann Tolbert, 57–75. Minneapolis: Fortress Press, 1995.

———. "Toward Intercultural Criticism: A Reading Strategy from the Diaspora." In *Reading from This Place: Social Location and Biblical Interpretation in Global Perspective*, edited by Fernando F. Segovia and Mary Ann Tolbert, 305–31. Minneapolis: Fortress Press, 1995.

Segovia, Fernando F., and Mary Ann Tolbert, eds. *Reading from This Place: Social Location and Biblical Interpretation in Global Perspective*. Volume 2. Minneapolis: Fortress Press, 1995.

————, eds. *Reading from This Place: Social Location and Biblical Interpretation in the United States.* Volume 1. Minneapolis: Fortress Press, 1995.

Shea, William H. "The Parallel Literary Structure of Revelation 12 and 20." *Andrews University Seminary Studies* 23 (1985): 37–54.

Smith, Abraham. "'I Saw the Book Talk': A Cultural Studies Approach to the Ethics of an African American Biblical Hermeneutic." *Semeia* 77 (1997): 115–38.

Smith, Jonathan Z. "Cross-Cultural Reflections on Apocalypticism." In *Ancient and Modern Perspectives on the Bible and Culture: Essays in Honor of Hans Dieter Betz,* edited by Adela Yarbro Collins, 281–85. Atlanta: Scholars Press, 1998.

Smith, Theophus. *Conjuring Culture: Biblical Formations of Black America.* New York and Oxford: Oxford University Press, 1994.

Spencer, Jon Michael. "Introduction." *Black Sacred Music: A Journal of Theomusicology* 6, no. 1 (1992): 265–67.

————. *Re-Searching Black Music.* Knoxville: University of Tennessee Press, 1996.

Steedman, Carolyn. "Culture, Cultural Studies, and the Historians." In *Cultural Studies,* edited by Lawrence Grossberg, Cary Nelson, and Paula A. Treichler, 613–21. New York and London: Routledge Press, 1992.

Storey, John. *Cultural Studies and the Study of Popular Culture: Theories and Methods.* Athens: University of Georgia Press, 1996.

————. "Cultural Studies: An Introduction." In *What is Cultural Studies? A Reader,* edited by John Storey, 1–13. London: Arnold Press, 1996.

————, ed. *Cultural Theory and Popular Culture: A Reader.* London: Harvester Wheatsheaf, 1994.

————. "Introduction: The Study of Popular Culture within Cultural Studies." In *Cultural Theory and Popular Culture: A Reader,* edited by John Storey, vii–xii. London: Harvester & Wheatsheaf, 1994.

————, ed. *What Is Cultural Studies? A Reader.* London: Arnold Press, 1996.

Strathmann, H. μάρτυς, μαρτυρέω, μαρτυρία. . . ." *TDNT* 4: 474–514.

Sugirtharajah, R. S. "A Brief Memorandum on Postcolonialism and Biblical Studies." *JSNT* 73 (1999): 3–5.

————. "Imperial Critical Commentaries: Christian Discourse and Commentarial Writings in Colonial India." *JSNT* 73 (1999): 83–112.

Terrell, JoAnn Marie. *Power in the Blood? The Cross in the African American Experience.* Maryknoll, NY: Orbis Books, 1998.

Trites, Allison A. "*Martus* and Martyrdom in the Apocalypse: A Semantic Study." *Novum Testamentum* 15 (1973): 72–80.

Volf, Miroslav. *Exclusion and Embrace: A Theological Exploration of Identity, Otherness, and Reconciliation.* Nashville: Abingdon Press, 1996.

Wainwright, Arthur. *Mysterious Apocalypse: A History of the Interpretation of the Book of Revelation.* Nashville: Abingdon Press, 1993.

Ward, Ewing. *The Power of the Lamb: Revelation's Theology of Liberation for You.* Cambridge, MA: Cowley Publishers, 1990.

West, Cornel. "On Afro-American Popular Music: From Bebop to Rap." *Black Sacred Music: A Journal of Theomusicology* 6, no. 1 (1992): 282–94.

Williams, Delores. "A Crucifixion Double Cross?" *Other Side* 29, no. 5 (September-October 1993): 25–27.

———. *Sisters in the Wilderness: The Challenge of Womanist God-Talk.* Maryknoll, NY: Orbis Books, 1993.

Wilmore, Gayraud. *Black Religion and Black Radicalism: An Interpretation of the Religious History of African Americans,* 3rd Edition. Maryknoll, NY: Orbis Books, 1998.

Wimberly, Edward P. "The Cross-Culturally Sensitive Reader." *Journal of the ITC* 25 (1998): 170–87.

Scripture and Ancient Source Index

Name and Subject Index

Bonhoeffer, Dietrich, 34
Boring, Eugene, 105–7
Brahmo Samaj, 17
Brer Rabbit, 101
Broadbent, Ralph, 12–13, 16–17

Caesar, 16, 38, 54, 61, 82, 87–88,
    103–5, 111
Cain, black as, 73
Centre for Contemporary Cultural
    Studies, Birmingham, 18–21
Christ, 41, 60, 73, 86, 89, 92, 113
    allegiance to, 88
    believers in, 52
    crucifixion of, 73
    imitation of, 72
    knowledge of, 73
    lordship of, 27, 48–49, 52, 54–55,
        63, 105
    as a mighty Lion, 86
    powerful and present, 1
    ransomed by, 104
    resurrection of, 57
    surrogacy of, 74
    symbol, 74
Christianity
    African American, 79
    American evangelicalism, 72
    British, 17
    Constantinian, 92
    first-century, 114
    heart of, 33
    Jamaican, 20
    social form of, 43
    Western, 65
Christians, ix, 33–34, 41, 46–48, 54,
    63, 71–73, 80, 88, 115
    African American, vii–viii, 36, 41,
        54–55, 59, 64, 77, 97
    enjoying the fruits of injustice, 32
    in the first century, x
    Indian, 17
    nonaccommodating, 87–88

persecution of, ix, 4, 87
    in the twenty-first century, x
    upbraiding John, 32, 34
church, viii, 110
    African American, ix, 18, 43, 66 (*see
        also* Black Church)
    of martyrs, ix
    metaphorical, 61–62, 64
civil rights movement, 22, 43, 64,
    83–85, 99
Civil Rights Act (1875), 95
Collins, Adela Yabro, 27, 29, 38–39,
    45, 52
colonialism, 25
commentaries
    African American, 18
    British, 16–17
community, 12, 15, 98
    African American, 41, 65, 85
    check to interpretation, 24, 35
    as "cultured," 8
    "from below," 22
    past and present, 5, 10
Cone, James, 44, 75, 85, 94–95,
    97, 108
context
    contemporary cultural, 40–45
    economic, ix
    first-century, 25
    historical, 4, 42
    as key, 40–49
    literary, 40
    political, ix
    social, ix
criticism
    biblical, 13, 21
    cultural, 23
    "higher," 26
    historical and literary, 13, 17,
        21–23, 35
    ideological, 9, 18–21, 26, 29, 31
cross, 33, 47, 60, 64, 70, 73–74,
    76–77, 81–82, 94